Brilliant Activities for Reading Non-fiction

Comprehension Activities for 7–11 Year Olds

May Stevenson

 Brilliant Publications

If you and your class enjoyed using the ideas in this book, you might be interested in the other books in the series:

Brilliant Activities for Reading Fiction   978-903853-45-0
Brilliant Activities for Persuasive Writing   978-903853-54-2

For more information on these and other books in the series, please contact us at the address given below.

Acknowledgement
The publishers and author are most grateful to Paula Goodridge for her excellent editing and comments.

Published by Brilliant Publications
Sales and despatch:
    BEBC Brilliant Publications
    Albion Close, Parkstone, Poole, Dorset BH12 3LL
    Tel: 0845 1309200 / 01202 712910
    Fax: 0845 1309300
    e-mail: brilliant@bebc.co.uk
    website: www.brilliantpublications.co.uk
Editorial and marketing:
    1 Church View, Sparrow Hall Farm, Edlesborough, Dunstable,
    Bedfordshire LU6 2ES

The name Brilliant Publications and its logo are registered trade marks.

Written by May Stevenson
Illustrated by Frank Endersby
Cover designed and illustrated by Lynda Murray
Copyright © May Stevenson 2006

ISBN: 978-1-903853-46-7

First published in 2006
10 9 8 7 6 5 4 3 2 1

Contents

Introduction

Brilliant Activities for Reading Non-fiction adds to the teaching of reading and writing by providing materials to develop Key Stage 2 children's ability to recognize different genres and styles in texts.

Within these activities the children will encounter a range of text types, including:

a) reference books on topics of interest

b) thesauruses

c) dictionaries with and without illustrations

d) instructions

e) letters written for a range of purposes: to recount, explain, congratulate, complain, etc.

f) alphabetical texts: directories, encyclopedias, indexes, etc.

g) reports and articles in newspapers and magazines

h) explanations and persuasive writing: adverts, circulars and flyers

i) accounts of events

j) rules, recipes, directions and notices

The activities are compatible with the Primary Literacy Strategy and may be carried out in the time allocated for the Literacy Hour. Each chapter contains instructions for teachers, texts and differentiated worksheets. Many of the chapters have extension activities.

1. Fact or fiction?

Aim

The children will understand the distinction between fact and fiction. They will be able to use the terms 'fact' and 'fiction' appropriately. They will understand what 'non-fiction' means.

Activities

Divide the children into groups according to ability. Ask the children for some examples of things that are true and things that are made up. Write these on the board under the headings 'fact' and 'fiction', and discuss them until the children understand the difference between the two terms.

Distribute sheet **1a** to the less able children and sheet **1b** to the more able. As a class, ask the children to look at the four examples of fact and fiction sentences. Discuss each one and ensure that they understand the concept. Tell the children that they are now going to work independently.

After approximately 20 minutes, go through all the sentences on the worksheets and check the children's answers to ensure they have understood. Ask for a few more examples of fact and fiction from the children and write them on the board.

Ask the children to write sentences on their own containing something that is fact and then something that is fiction.

Plenary

Bring the children together again and go over the sentences they have written with them.

Look at various fiction and non-fiction books with the children. Pick out sentences from them and ask whether they are fact or fiction. Explain that fiction books are story books, and non-fiction books are books about facts. Have a range of different non-fiction books for the children to look at, including reference books, dictionaries and information books.

Fact or fiction?

Name: ....

Fact:	Fiction:
A **fact** is something that is true like "Spiders have eight legs."	**Fiction** is a made-up story like "The cow jumped over the moon."

| **Fact**: Light travels in a straight line. | **Fiction**: The witch's cottage was made of cake and sweets. |

Read these sentences and write beside each one whether you think it is fact or fiction:

1. Some people ride horses. _____

2. Hens lay eggs. _____

3. A bus can fly. _____

4. Trees can talk. _____

5. Lions live in kennels. _____

6. Fish live in water. _____

Fact or fiction?

Name: ....

Fact:	Fiction:
A **fact** is something that is true like "Spiders have eight legs."	**Fiction** is a made-up story like "The cow jumped over the moon."

Fact: Light travels in a straight line.	**Fiction**: The witch's cottage was made of cake and sweets.

Read these sentences and write beside each one whether you think it is fact or fiction:

1. A dragon-fly is an insect with six legs. _____

2. The Gingerbread Man said, "You can't catch me." _____

3. Hedgehogs hibernate in winter. _____

4. Bears eat bowls of porridge for breakfast. _____

5. The main stem of a tree is called a trunk. _____

6. Nellie the elephant packed her trunk. _____

Extension activity

Write at least six facts about yourself.

2. About balloons

Aim

The children will compare two pieces of writing and note the differences in the style and purpose of fiction and non-fiction writing.

Activities

Put the children into two groups according to ability.

Have some pictures of balloons and hot air balloons on display. Let the children talk about them and about their own experiences of balloons.

Distribute sheet **2a** to the less able readers and sheet **2b** to the more able.

Read the passages with the whole class and ask if they can see any differences between them. Put some of their answers on the board. Ask the children how many adjectives they can find in the two passages. Show that **A** is non-fiction because it contains facts about balloons and it only uses one adjective which is needed to describe how a balloon is made.

Ask the children what we learn about both Tom and the balloon's feelings in the second passage. Could this happen in real life? Explain that **B** is fiction because it is part of a story. It contains adjectives to help us picture things. It talks about Tom's feelings, and even attributes feelings to the balloon and allows it to speak.

Ask the children to answer the questions on their sheet.

Plenary

Gather the children together again. Go through answers, checking that all the children have identified the fact and fiction passages correctly. Discuss the use of adjectives and descriptive verbs. Why do the children think these two passages were written?

Listen to the story endings the children have written.

About balloons

Name: ....

A A balloon is a rubber bag filled with gas which makes it rise into the air. A hot-air balloon has a basket under it for passengers to travel in.

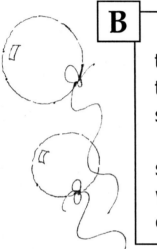

B Tom lovingly tied the large balloon to the table beside his bed. When he was asleep, the balloon tugged angrily on the string and suddenly it was floating free.

"That's better," it whispered with a sly smile. Then it swayed towards the open window and squeezed out into the cool evening.

1. Which word tells us that Tom loved the balloon?

2. Which words tell us that the balloon did not love Tom?

3. What do you think might happen to the balloon?

About balloons

Name: ....

A A balloon is a rubber bag filled with gas which makes it rise into the air. A hot-air balloon has a basket under it for passengers to travel in.

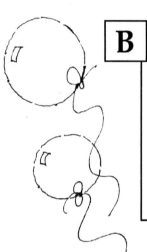

B Tom lovingly tied the large balloon to the table beside his bed. When he was asleep, the balloon tugged angrily on the string and suddenly it was floating free.

"That's better," it whispered with a sly smile. Then it swayed towards the open window and squeezed out into the cool evening.

1. In what kind of book might you find passage **A**?

2. Where would you be likely to find passage **B**?

3. Which word tells us that Tom loved the balloon?

4. Do you think that the balloon loved Tom? Why?

Extension activity
Write a short story about what you think might happen next in passage **B**. Use the other side of this sheet if you need to.

3. Finding information

Aim

The children will find information in reference books. They will be familiar with terms relating to the different sections in them and understand how to look things up in the contents and index.

Activities

Put the children into mixed ability groups and issue each group with some books which contain a contents page and an index. Discuss the terms 'contents', 'index', 'headings', 'sub-headings', 'page numbers' and 'bibliography'.

Give the children several topics to look up in the contents. For example, in a book about animals in the countryside you might ask them to look for the chapter on birds. Then ask them to find the index and look up some specific bird names that they know, or give them some examples. Do this several times with different topics. When the children seem comfortable with what they are doing, split them into two groups according to ability.

Distribute sheet **3a** to the less able children and sheet **3b** to the more able.

Go over sheet **3a** with the less able children and give help where needed.

Plenary

Bring the children together again and check their answers. Ask them which chapter in the contents page on their worksheet they think will be the most interesting.

Finding information

Name: ....

Match the words in the **Index** to the correct chapter from the **Contents** page. An example has been done for you. Some words in the Index might appear in more than one chapter.

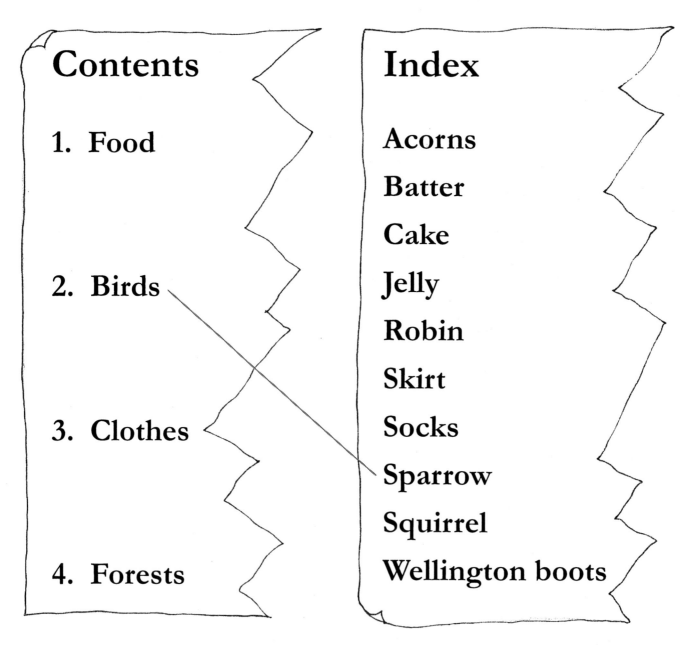

Contents

1. Food

2. Birds

3. Clothes

4. Forests

Index

Acorns

Batter

Cake

Jelly

Robin

Skirt

Socks

Sparrow

Squirrel

Wellington boots

Finding information

Name: ....

In the **Contents** page of a children's encyclopedia the following chapters are listed:

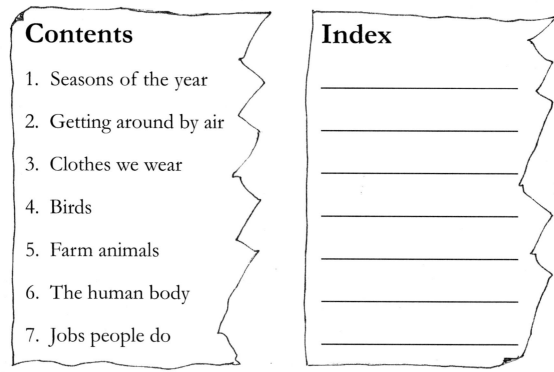

Contents

1. Seasons of the year

2. Getting around by air

3. Clothes we wear

4. Birds

5. Farm animals

6. The human body

7. Jobs people do

Index

_____

_____

_____

_____

_____

_____

_____

Here is a list of words found in the **Index**:

Aeroplane
Coat
Nose
Sheep
Sparrow
Spring
Teacher

1. In the **Index** column write each word beside the right chapter in the **Contents** column. For example, "Spring" should be written beside "Seasons of the year".

2. Use the Contents and Index pages of a book to find out five facts about something which interests you, such as an animal.

4. Making faces

Aim

The children will read an information passage and identify the main points, by underlining key words and phrases, and use these points to answer questions. They will also see how facts can be found in reference books.

Activities

Have some reference books about any topic relating to humans available for the class to look at.

The class can all work together on sheet **4a**. Read the passage then ask what it is about. Ask the children to underline the four things we do with our faces. Then ask them to complete the worksheet, and go over the answers as a class.

Ask the children to look at sheet **4b** and write down as many facts as they can about human beings. As an extension activity, those who finish early can look for some more facts about people in reference books.

Plenary

Bring the class together again and go over their examples. Write some facts on the board. Ask those who found additional facts in books to show where they are from to the rest of the class.

Making faces

Name: ....

Did you know that we often tell other people how we are feeling without saying a word? If we are surprised we will raise our eyebrows. When we are angry we pull our eyebrows close together. If we are happy we smile. When we cannot decide about something we might frown.

Now answer these questions. What might we do when:

1. We are surprised?

2. We are angry?

3. We are happy?

4. We cannot decide about something?

Facts about human beings

Name: ....

Write down some fascinating facts about human beings:

1. _A human being can be male or female._

2. _____

3. _____

4. _____

5. _____

6. _____

7. _____

8. _____

9. _____

10. _____

11. _____

12. _____

Extension activity

Look at some information books to find more facts about people.

5. Different purposes of writing

Aim

The children will identify and understand different types of instructional texts, where they might appear and their purpose.

Activities

As a class discuss the need for instructional writing such as recipes, timetables or instructions. Ask the children to name any they know and why they are used. Discuss school rules and why they are in place. Ask if they know of any other rules outside of school which they should obey, for example, at road crossings, in board games, etc.

Divide the class into two or more groups according to ability. Give sheet **5a** to the whole class and help the less able to complete it. Give the more able children sheet **5b** to complete after they finish sheet **5a**.

Plenary

Discuss the answers to sheet **5a**, making sure that the children have understood what they were doing. Write some of the children's rules on the board and have a discussion about them.

Read the passage on worksheet **5b** to the whole class and ask the children who completed it to give their answers. Ask for contributions from the rest of the class.

Extension activity

Ask the children to take turns at reading the instructions for 'Jamie's board game' on sheet **5c** and then answer the questions. Go over their answers as a class.

Different purposes of writing

Name: ....

A 1. Mix icing sugar with a few drops of water.
2. Add some peppermint essence.
3. Form into shapes and leave to harden.

B The Glasgow train leaves at five minutes past every hour.

C Pupils must **always** walk in single file on the stairs!

1. In which kind of book would you find text **A**?

2. Where would you see the information in text **B**?

3. Why do you think the notice in text **C** would be put up?

4. Make a list of rules you would like to see used either in school or at home:

   1. _____

   2. _____

   3. _____

   4. _____

Name: ....

A Guide to Healthy Eating

1. Eat at least five portions of fruit and vegetables every day. You can eat them raw or cooked.
2. Save cakes, sweets and crisps for special treats.
3. We get milk and meat from animals. They have lots of protein to help us grow big and strong. Eating eggs, fish and cheese is good for us too.

---

1. Write down three things that you think are healthy foods.

2. Write down three foods that you think are not so healthy.

3. What foods need to be cooked? Write down three.

4. What can we eat raw?

5. Write three kinds of food we get from animals.

6. What don't you like to eat?

Jamie's action game

Name: ....

1. You need a starting line and a finishing line.

I've made up a game! Here are the rules.

2. You need three players, and three tokens marked **A**, **B** and **C**.

3. Each player picks a token out of a bag and they all line up at the start.

4. The player with token **A** decides whether all the players should **hop**, take a **step** or **jump**. Everyone does this.

5. Then the player with token **B** decides which action he wants everyone to do next.

Hop!

6. Then the player with token **C** chooses **two** of the movements for everyone to do (e.g. a jump followed by a hop).

Step!

7. Repeat steps 4–6 until the first player crosses the finishing line. This person is the winner.

Jump!

1. Without trying the game say whether you think it is fair or not.

2. What might make it fairer?

3. In what ways do you think the game would be good for you?

4. Try the game some time and see what you think!

6. Following instructions

Aim

The children will read and understand some simple instructions. They will understand that instructions are usually given for a good reason.

Activities

Have a discussion with the whole class about when they might come across instructions, written and oral. Take examples, e.g. dinner hall procedures, school rules, building instructions for toys and home appliances, etc. Discuss what might happen to you if you ignored these instructions.

If you have one available, use a large book to read and discuss an instructional text together.

Tell the children that they are going to complete a worksheet on instructions, then separate them into two groups by ability. Hand out sheet **6a** to the less able group and **6b** to the more able group. Give the children time to complete their tasks, helping where necessary.

Plenary

Gather the class together again. Go through the questions, alternating between the groups and discuss their answers. Remind them about how useful instructions can be and that they should always be looked at carefully.

Following instructions

Name: ....

For your safety and comfort:

1. You should always wear a helmet when riding a bicycle.

2. In very cold weather you should wear extra clothes.

3. If you are painting you should wear an apron.

---

1. Why should you wear a helmet when riding a bicycle?

2. Why should you wear extra clothes in the winter?

3. What does an apron do for you when you are painting?

Extension activity

On the back of this sheet write down some instructions to tell someone how to make a snowman.

Following instructions

Name: ....

Here are some simple instructions for getting your own breakfast:

1.	Place a bowl and spoon on a table.
2.	Pour some cereal carefully into the bowl.
3.	Close the cereal packet.
4.	Pour some milk onto the cereal.
5.	Put the milk back into the fridge.

1. Five things could go wrong if you did not follow these simple instructions. Write them down. The first one has been done for you:

a) *If the bowl is not on a flat surface the cereal might spill.*

b) _____

c) _____

d) _____

e) _____

On a bottle of cough mixture it gives the correct dose:

Children 6–12 years:
One 5ml spoonful every 4–6 hours.
Children over 12 years:
Two 5ml spoonfuls every 4–6 hours.

2. How many spoonfuls should these children take every 4–6 hours?

a) A girl of ten _____

b) A boy of thirteen _____

c) A boy of two _____

Extension activity
Write a set of instructions for someone entitled 'How to make a sandwich'.

7. Letter writing

Aim

The children will read examples of letters written for a range of purposes. They will discuss the format of a letter and note different ways of starting and finishing it. They will also understand how the style of a letter varies depending on who it is written to, and the differences between formal and informal letters.

Activities

Discuss letter writing with the children. When might they want to write a letter rather than telephone or send an e-mail? Why? Who might prefer letters to e-mails? Do they like receiving letters? How many different reasons can they think of for writing letters (e.g. to thank someone, to complain, to make an enquiry, to congratulate)?

Hand out sheet **7a** and read the text. Discuss its content. Who is it to? Why was it written? What does the writer ask for? Is it polite? Then discuss the format, noting the address, date, "Dear Sir/Madam", "Yours faithfully" and signature, and where each of these is positioned.

Ask the children for appropriate beginnings to other letters, e.g. to a friend, a relative or a teacher. Point out that some of these letters should be formal and some informal.

Divide the children into two groups according to ability. Give the less able children sheet **7b** and ask them to complete it, discussing it with them first if needed. Give the more able children sheet **7c**. When they complete it, they can try sheet **7d**.

Plenary

Bring the class together again and discuss their answers to ensure that they have understood.

Extension activity

Ask the children to write a short letter of their own.

7 Bond Road
Andover
Bodshire
AL3 6OP

19th February 2008

Dear Sir/Madam,

I am writing to complain about the computer game I bought from your shop last Saturday. When I got home it did not work, so I am sending it back to you with a copy of the receipt.

Please can you send me a new game or refund my money?

I look forward to hearing from you.

Yours faithfully,

IMA Moaner

Mrs. I.M.A. Moaner

© May Stevenson

This page may be photocopied for use by the purchasing institution only.

Brilliant Activities for Reading Non-fiction

25

Letter writing

Name: ....

A

5 Smith Street
Ayr
A36 1AB

Friday 22nd June

Dear Great Aunt Margaret,
    Thank you very much for my birthday present. It will be very useful.
    I hope you are keeping well.

Love from Amy xx

B

Sunday

Hi Mark – Sorry you missed the trip to Edinburgh, but I've taken photos for you and got you a present. Hope your throat is better now.

See you soon,

Nasif

1. Which letter is formal?

2. Which is informal?

3. What was wrong with Mark?

Extension activity

Write a thank-you letter to an imaginary aunt or uncle.

Letter writing

Name: ....

A

24 High Crescent
Glasgow
GL3 6BR
22nd January 2007

Dear Miss Wilson,
     Elliot is not a lazy boy
and he is not a bully.
     He is unhappy because
he cannot get peace to finish
his work and that is why he
sometimes hits the others.
     I hope that you will note
the things I have said and
that you will try to make
things more enjoyable for
him.

          Yours sincerely,

          M Brown

          Mrs M Brown

B

Wednesday

Simone – What are you
like? Fancy winning the
sports championship! I
never knew that you
could run so fast or jump
so high. Well done! We'll
have to meet up and have
a chat about it.

     Luv,
          Jane x

1. Which letter makes a complaint?

2. Which letter congratulates?

3. What is different between the beginning of letter A and of letter B?

4. What does this tell us about the people they were writing to?

Extension activity
Write a letter of complaint to someone.

Letter writing

Name: ....

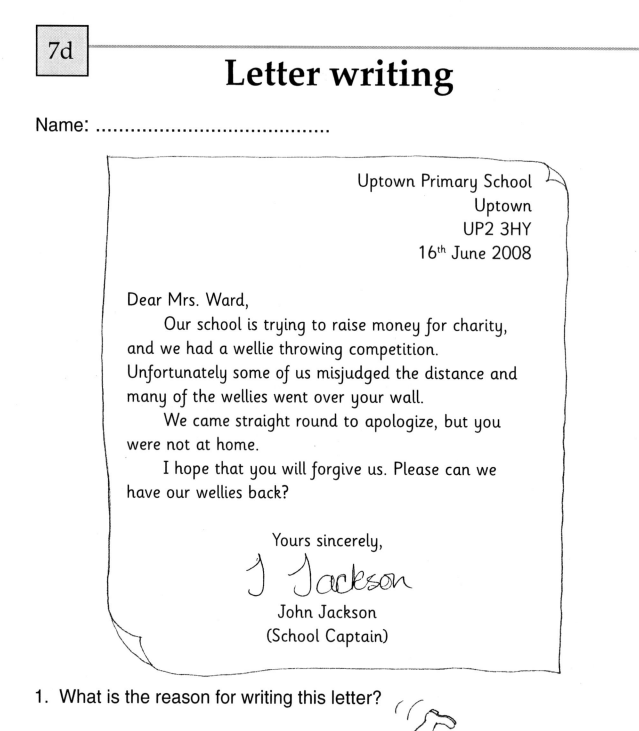

Uptown Primary School
Uptown
UP2 3HY
16th June 2008

Dear Mrs. Ward,

  Our school is trying to raise money for charity, and we had a wellie throwing competition. Unfortunately some of us misjudged the distance and many of the wellies went over your wall.

  We came straight round to apologize, but you were not at home.

  I hope that you will forgive us. Please can we have our wellies back?

Yours sincerely,

J Jackson

John Jackson
(School Captain)

1. What is the reason for writing this letter?

2. Why do you think it was John Jackson who had to write this letter?

3. Is this a formal or informal letter?

8. Understanding what you read

Aim

The children will read a passage in the style of a newspaper article and look at how it is laid out. They will also try to summarize its contents in one sentence and find the main point it is making.

Activities

Read the two passages on sheet **8a** to the class. Then divide the children into two groups according to ability and hand the sheet out to all of them. Ask the less able children to read passage **A**, and the more able to read passage **B**.

Discuss the layout of the articles. Explain what a headline is. Can the children think of alternative headlines for these articles? Point out that the first paragraph is bolder than the others. Why do the children think this might be? Show that the headline, bold opening paragraph and picture all help to grab the reader's attention and encourage them to read on.

Make sure that the less able children have fully understood their passage and then give them sheet **8b**. Give the more able group sheet **8c**. Ask the children to answer the questions on their sheet, giving help where needed.

Plenary

Bring the class together again. Read passage **A** to the class and then ask for volunteers to read out their one sentence summary of it. Ask others what they think the main point was.

Do the same with passage **B** and take oral answers from the pupils concerned.

Understanding what you read

A BOY INJURED BY FIREWORK

An eight-year-old boy is in hospital after being badly burned at a firework party.

Kevin Williams was with his family at a bonfire party in his garden last Saturday when the accident happened.

The police have reported that Kevin threw a firework, probably a rocket, onto the fire while his parents were busy handing out sparklers.

"We warned him to be careful and not go near the fireworks," says Mrs. Williams. "I think he got over-excited and forgot what we said."

B BOY RUN OVER AT PARK

A six-year-old boy is in hospital after being hit by a car next to Silverton Park.

On Thursday of last week, Jack Olivers was knocked over by a passing car after running out into the road. He is in St. Matthews Hospital and is currently in a stable condition.

The accident happened when an ice-cream van stopped in Lemon Street opposite the park gates. Jack is reported to have run across the road towards the van, without looking to see if any cars were coming.

Local residents have often complained about the fact that the busy Lemon Street runs so close to the park. However, the Council has not made any plans to improve the area and make it safer for children.

Understanding what you read

Name: ....

Read newspaper article **A** and then try to answer these questions:

1. What was Kevin warned about?

2. What did Kevin do wrong?

3. What happened next?

4. Try telling the story in one sentence.

5. What is the main point of this article?

Understanding what you read

Name: ....

Read newspaper article **B** and then complete the questions below:

1. What is the article about?

2. Where does it take place?

3. What happens first?	4. What happens next?
5. Then what happens?	6. What happens after that?

7. Why are the local residents unhappy?

8. Try telling the story in one sentence.

9. What do you think is the main point of the article?

9. Fact or opinion?

Aim

The pupils will understand and use the terms 'fact' and 'opinion'. They will distinguish between sentences that are fact or opinion and provide their own examples.

Activities

Write 'fiction' and 'non-fiction' on the board. Produce examples of fiction and non-fiction books and ask the children to tell you which are fiction and which are non-fiction.

Remind the children that non-fiction books usually contain facts. Ask for some examples of facts they might find in reference books, dictionaries, newspapers, etc.

Ask the children whether everything in a newspaper is fact. Show them an example of a newspaper article containing somebody's opinion.

Write 'fact' and 'opinion' on the board. Ask for some examples of facts and write them under 'fact'. Do the same with some opinions.

Distribute sheet **9a** to the less able pupils and sheet **9b** to the more able. Read the definitions of fact and opinion to both groups and then ask them to complete the sheets, helping where necessary.

Plenary

Bring the class together and discuss answers from both groups, emphasizing that opinion is a feeling which may or may not be true. Take further examples orally of facts and opinions. Ask the children how our opinions sometimes affect our behaviour. Ask for examples of how this can be positive or negative.

Fact or opinion?

Name: ....

A **fact** is something that is true. An **opinion** is a feeling you have about something or someone which is based on your belief or judgement, but may or may not be true. For example: 'There are seven days in a week' is a **fact**. 'Fish is tasty' is an **opinion**.

1. Read the list below and beside each one tick whether you think it is **fact** or **opinion**:

	Fact	Opinion
a) Butter tastes nice.		
b) Football is boring.		
c) Yellow is a colour.		
d) School is fun.		
e) London is a large city.		
f) Tomatoes are delicious.		
g) Girls are cleverer than boys.		
h) Cod is a fish.		

2. Write down one thing that is a **fact** and one that is an **opinion**:

Fact: _____

_____

Opinion: _____

_____

Fact or opinion?

Name: ....

A **fact** is something that is true. An **opinion** is a feeling you have about something or someone which is based on your belief or judgement, but may or may not be true. For example: 'There are seven days in a week' is a **fact**. 'Fish is tasty' is an **opinion**.

---

1. Below are some things said by pupils in the playground. Read the list and beside each one tick whether you think it is **fact** or **opinion**:

	Fact	Opinion
a) Jamil has brown eyes.		
b) Nobody likes soup.		
c) The pop star loves his fans.		
d) The football team is rubbish.		
e) We need pencils at school.		
f) March has 31 days.		

2. Write down some of your own facts and opinions:

Facts	**Opinions**
_____	_____
_____	_____
_____	_____
_____	_____

10. Newspaper headlines

Aim

The children will discuss newspaper headlines and how they are used. They will look at two headlines and predict newspaper stories to go with them, making notes or writing a summary, and then checking these against the original. They will realize that journalists sometimes play with words to make a headline more dramatic.

Activities

Display a newspaper page in front of the children and ask them to point to the headlines. Ask them what the headlines are there for. Divide the children into groups according to ability. Have a variety of different newspaper headlines for the children to look at and talk about in their group. Make sure that the content matches their maturity!

Hand out sheet **10a** to the whole class. Let them discuss in their groups what the articles might be about. Then ask each child to write ideas or a short summary of what they think each article will be about. The less able can just complete the first one.

Give the children sheet **10b** and ask them to read the articles. Ensure that all the children understand the articles and go over any unfamiliar words. Then hear as many as possible of their own ideas and summaries. Which story was harder to guess from the headline? How does the writer of the second article play with the word "shocking"? What did the children understand by the word at first? Why do they think the journalist did this?

Ask each child to write some more headlines of their own. Remind them that headlines should be short and attention-grabbing. Can they play with words to make them more interesting?

Plenary

As a whole class, discuss the children's headlines and what stories might be written about them. Which headlines would make them want to read on?

Extension activity

Ask each child to swap headlines with a friend and write a story to go with it. Hear these as a class and discuss.

Newspaper headlines

Name: ....

Look at the two headlines written below. Beneath each headline write your ideas or a summary of what you think each one is about.

MOUNTAIN RESCUE

_____

_____

_____

_____

_____

_____

"SHOCKING" SCHOOL CLOSES

_____

_____

_____

_____

_____

_____

Brilliant Activities for Reading Non-fiction

Newspaper headlines

Name: ....

Here are the stories behind the headlines on sheet **10a**. Read these and then compare them with the ones you have written.

MOUNTAIN RESCUE

Police and the local mountain rescue team were called out yesterday to search for a young boy who had walked away from his party and then could not be found in the mist. We are glad to report that after a long search the boy was found uninjured.

"SHOCKING" SCHOOL CLOSES

Booling Primary School was closed for two days so that workmen could replace furniture which was giving off electric shocks when touched with wet hands. No one was injured, but a man from the Council commented, "This is a shocking case!"

How did your stories compare? Make up headlines of your own and write them on the back of the sheet.

Extension activity

Swap one of your headlines with a friend's and write a report to go with their headline.

11. Painting class

Aim

The children will read a piece of instructional text where the instructions are in the wrong order, and re-order them. They will recognize and note the materials needed and understand the sequential stages. They will understand the need for clarity in instructions and discuss the intended reader.

Activities

Put the children into mixed ability groups. Display the text from sheet **11a** on an interactive screen or overhead projector with the instructions in the wrong order. If you are unable to display the text, provide each group with the instructions cut up and mixed up. Read through the instructions as a class. If you are displaying the text, can the children see what is wrong with them?

Ask the children to decide in their groups what order the instructions should be in. Discuss the order as a class. Groups may disagree on where the last point should go – if so you can discuss this.

Hand out sheet **11a** to the whole class. Discuss the content and layout of the instructions. Why is it important to list the materials? Are the instructions clear? Who might use them?

Ask the children to complete sheet **11b** on their own. More able children could then write their own instructions for a reception teacher to use for his/her class (see extension activity).

Plenary

Bring the children back again and discuss their answers. What have they learnt about reading or writing instructions? Hear any instructions they have written and discuss them as a class.

Painting class

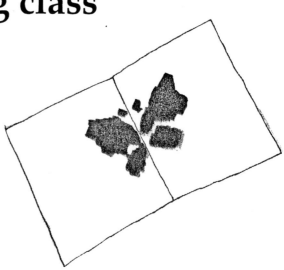

Paper butterflies

Materials
one sheet of A4 plain paper
red, yellow and blue paint
three paintbrushes

Instructions

1. Fold the sheet of paper in half then open it out like a birthday card.

2. On one side of the paper, near the fold and above the middle of the paper, put a blob of blue paint (about the size of a ten pence piece).

3. Underneath the blue blob, put a blob of yellow paint about five times the size, making sure that the two colours just touch.

4. Below the yellow blob, put a small blob of red paint, just touching the yellow paint.

5. Fold over the other half of the paper and press down for a few seconds then open the sheet out. You should have a colourful butterfly.

6. If you wish you can outline the butterfly shape with a felt tip pen.

7. You can mix and swirl your paints to make other, colourful butterflies.

Painting class

Name: ....

Answer these questions:

1. What materials do you need to make a butterfly?
2. What is the first thing you need to do?
3. After you put a blob of blue paint on, what do you do next?
4. After the blob of yellow paint, what do you do?
5. Which age group do you think the butterfly painting would appeal to the most?
6. Who might the instructions be useful to?

Extension activity

Think of another activity that children in a reception class would enjoy.
Write instructions for their teacher to use to explain what they need to
do.

12. Cookery class

Aim

The children will read an instructional text and discuss its layout and the sequential stages. They will identify and understand the language of commands.

Activities

Read the text on sheet **12a** together. What kind of text is it? What do the children notice about how the recipe is laid out? How does the title "Top hats" help the reader to understand the instructions? Why are the instructions numbered and not written out in paragraphs?

Ask the children what the first two instructions warn us about. Why is this helpful? How many commands can they find? Are the instructions clear?

Hand out sheet **12b** and give the children ten minutes to complete it. Give help to the less able as needed. Then ask the children to write their own recipe (extension activity).

Plenary

Bring the class together again and share their recipes.

Extension activity

Re-draft the children's recipes and put some on display, or make a class cookery book.

Cookery class

Top hats

Ingredients
one small block of cooking chocolate
one packet of marshmallows
one packet of chocolate beans

Equipment
non-metallic bowl
microwave
teaspoon
paper cake cases

Instructions
1. Wash and dry hands. Note: if your hands are not thoroughly dry when handling chocolate, it will turn white and crumbly.

2. Break the chocolate into squares and place it in a dry non-metallic bowl in the microwave. Heat until the chocolate is melted and runny. Note: watch the chocolate carefully to make sure it does not burn. Ask an adult to help you.

3. Drop a teaspoonful of liquid chocolate into a paper case. Place a marshmallow on top.

4. Dip a chocolate bean into the bowl of melted chocolate and place it on top of the marshmallow.

5. Repeat steps 3 and 4 with the remainder of the ingredients and leave the top hats to set. When the chocolate has hardened you can peel away the paper cake cases.

Cookery class

Name: ....

1. What ingredients do you need to make top hats?

2. What is the first thing you need to do?

3. What should you do next?

4. What is the last thing you need to do to your top hats?

5. Why is it useful to know what equipment you will need at the start?

Extension activity
Make up your own recipe for something delicious to sell at the school fête.

13. The class garden

Aim

The children will read some notes made for planning purposes and assess their usefulness. They will then transfer the information into a table.

Activities

Give every child sheet **13a** and discuss it, allowing children to contribute orally. Why do they think Sunil decided to make notes? Are there other things he needs to think about? Do the children have any other suggestions for him?

Give every child sheet **13b** and ask them to complete it. The more able children can then tackle sheet **13c**.

Plenary

Discuss the children's answers. Draw a table on the board similar to the one on sheet **13b**, and discuss as a class how you could fill it in for the task of putting plants into the garden. Why is this table useful for planning a task?

Extension activity

As a class, ask the children to make notes to help them plan a bring-and-buy sale for charity. Ask the children to use these notes to fill in a table for planning each task they will need to do.

The class garden

The children in Sunil's class are told they can make a small garden in the grassy area outside the classroom. Sunil has been asked to find out as much as he can about gardening and plan what they need to do. He has to think about what equipment they will need as well. He decides to make some notes for himself:

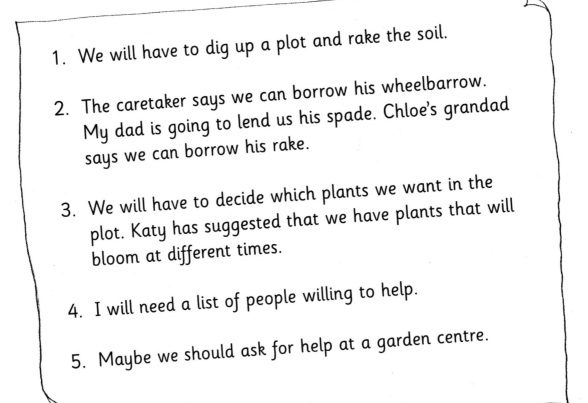

1. We will have to dig up a plot and rake the soil.

2. The caretaker says we can borrow his wheelbarrow. My dad is going to lend us his spade. Chloe's grandad says we can borrow his rake.

3. We will have to decide which plants we want in the plot. Katy has suggested that we have plants that will bloom at different times.

4. I will need a list of people willing to help.

5. Maybe we should ask for help at a garden centre.

The class garden

Name: ....

1. Sunil needs your help to decide how to go about the first task that needs doing in the class garden. Use the notes he made to help you to complete this table for him:

First task	Tools needed	Where to seek advice	Helpers
Dig up a plot and rake the soil.			

2. Why does Katy think it would be a good idea to have flowers that bloom at different times?

3. If Sunil asked you to be a helper, what might you be asked to do?

The class garden

Name: ....

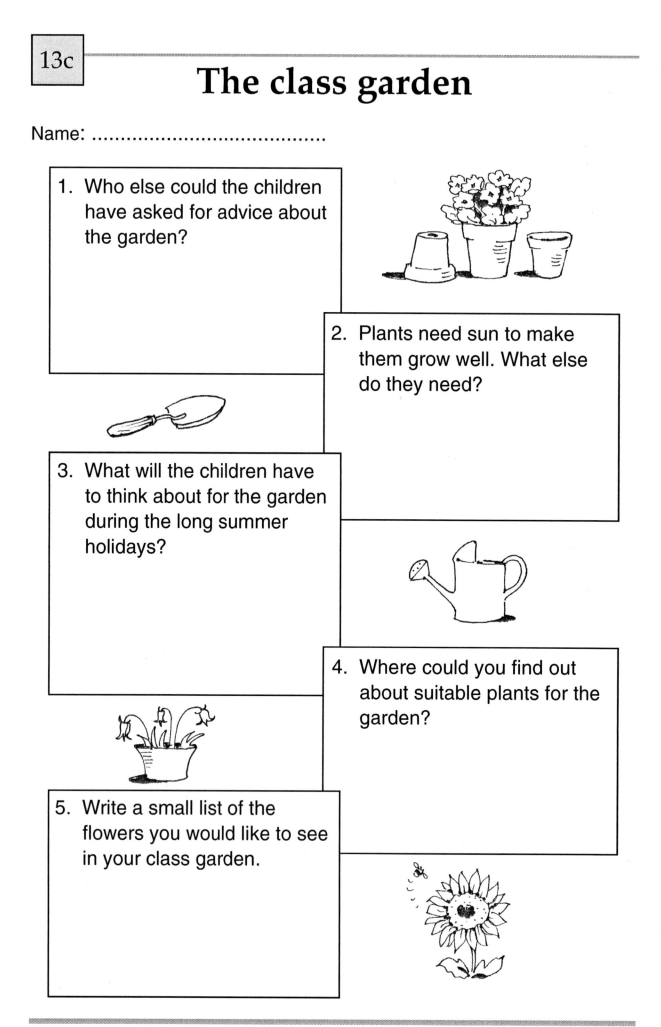

1. Who else could the children have asked for advice about the garden?

2. Plants need sun to make them grow well. What else do they need?

3. What will the children have to think about for the garden during the long summer holidays?

4. Where could you find out about suitable plants for the garden?

5. Write a small list of the flowers you would like to see in your class garden.

14. Staying alive

Aim

The children will scan a text to locate key words and phrases, and then use these as a tool for summarizing the text.

Activities

Have a discussion with the whole class as to where they think dangers lie in their lives and why. How do they avoid these dangers? What rules do adults make for them and why?

Hand out sheet **14a** and help the less able children to complete it.

Plenary

Listen to what the children have written and talk some more about it. Hear the responses to other things they may be hurt by and put some on the board. Point out that most dangers can be avoided by being careful. Ask some of the children to summarize the passage orally. Remind them that a summary should be brief but include the main points.

Extension activity

Children can use the list they made on sheet **14a** to write a short leaflet for parents advising them how to keep their children safe.

Staying alive

Name: ....

There are many things around us that could hurt us if we are not careful. Children are at risk every day on the roads, as traffic can be very dangerous. Fire and electricity can be harmful as well, and children need to learn to respect them. Accidents involving knives or stairs and injuries caused by medicines or chemicals can be avoided too.

Children should never talk to strangers unless it is someone they know they can trust, like a police officer. Talking to strangers on the internet is especially dangerous.

Making rules is a way of trying to protect children from these dangers. Parents and teachers make rules for children because they want to keep them safe and happy.

1. Make a list of all the things that could hurt you in the text above. Beside each one, write what you can do to avoid being hurt by it.

2. Write down any other things you think could harm you.

15. The largest lizard

Aim

The children will understand how and why paragraphs are used to organize and sequence information.

Activities

If possible have a picture of a Komodo dragon to show to the children. Write the name on the board, also write 'Indonesia'. Give the children sheet **15a** and read it as a class. Let them discuss it.

Tell the children to look at the content and placing of each paragraph and ask why they think the text is written in this way. How many paragraphs are there? Point out that each paragraph contains important information about the subject which might not be taken in so well if the whole text was written as one paragraph.

Give sheet **15b** to the less able children and sheet **15c** to the more able and ask them to answer the questions.

Plenary

Ask some children to look up Indonesia in an atlas or preferably on a globe of the world and let all the children see where it is.

Go over sheet **15b** and hear the children's answers. Then go over sheet **15c**, doing the same. Discuss where necessary.

Ask the children to draw their idea of a Komodo dragon, and display them.

Extension activity

Allow the children to use the internet to research Komodo dragons and Indonesia. Add this information to the display of their work.

The largest lizard

The largest known lizard in the world is the **Komodo dragon**. It has a heavy body, a long tail and very strong claws.

Komodo dragons can grow to be three metres long, but unlike fairy tale dragons they do not blow smoke or breathe fire!

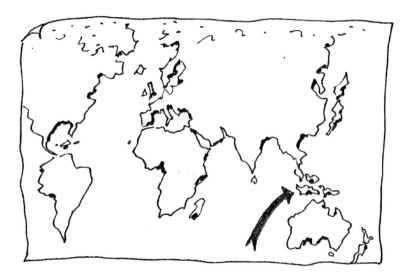

Try laying three metre sticks end to end on the floor and see how frightening it would be to meet this lizard.

Luckily for us, Komodo dragons only live on a few islands in Indonesia, including Komodo Island.

The largest lizard

Name: ....

1. What is the name of the lizard?

2. What length is the lizard?

3. Can this dragon blow smoke or breathe fire?

4. Where does the Komodo dragon live?

5. Why is it lucky for us that the dragon lives in Indonesia?

The largest lizard

Name: ....

1. Paragraph 1 tells us four things about the lizard. What are they?

a)

b)

c)

d)

2. Paragraph 2 tells us three more pieces of information. What are they?

a)

b)

c)

3. What will we find out if we do as paragraph 3 suggests?

4. Are we likely to find a Komodo dragon in the wild in our country? Why?

5. Why do you think this information is split into four paragraphs rather than written as one long piece?

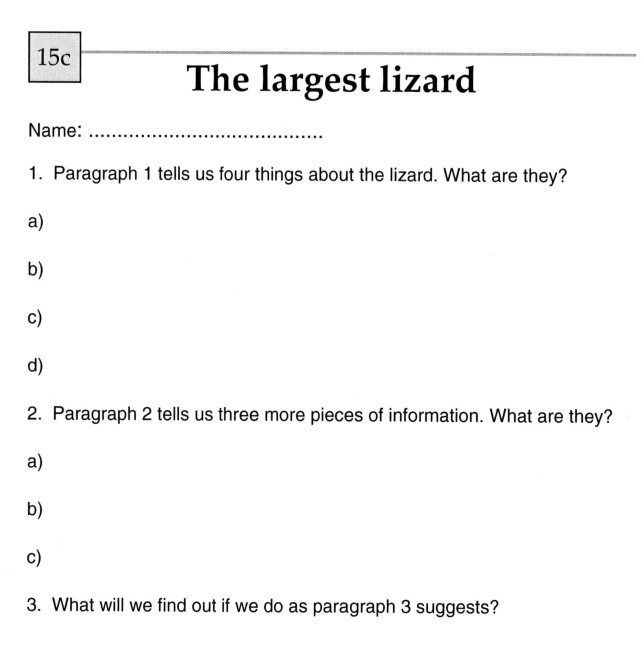

16. Making you buy

Aim

The children will recognize persuasive writing and investigate how style and vocabulary are used to convince the reader.

Activities

Hand out sheet **16a** and read the two adverts with the children as a whole class. Ask what appeals to them in these adverts. Which do they prefer? Would they buy from an advert like these? Why? Ask for examples of any adverts they know which might persuade them to buy something.

Read through the text in the first advert again. Ask the children why the advert uses words like "latest", "hottest", "pretty" and "trendiest". What does "lotsa" mean? Why is it used here? Read through the second advert again. Why does it use words like "gear", "trendiest" and "wow"? Why is the shop name spelt "Kidz"? In both adverts, why are some of the words bigger and bolder than the rest? Why are there lots of exclamation marks?

Ask the children to complete sheet **16b**. Give help to less able pupils.

Ask the children to make an advert of their own which they think would persuade people to buy something.

Plenary

As a class, listen to some of the children's answers to the worksheet. Hear as many as possible of the adverts they have produced. Ask the children to bring in any commercial adverts which appeal to them and display them.

Making you buy

Below are two different advertisements. Read them and then answer the questions on your worksheet.

Making you buy

Name: ....

1. What in the adverts would make children want to buy **PRETTY** magazine or clothes from **KIDZ**? Fill in the table:

❋ PRETTY ❋	⚽ KIDZ ⚽

2. What would make parents want to buy **PRETTY** magazine or clothes from **KIDZ**? Fill in the table:

❋ PRETTY ❋	⚽ KIDZ ⚽

17. Advertising

Aim

The children will evaluate several adverts for their impact and appeal, focusing on how information about the product is presented. They will note tactics for grabbing attention, linguistic devices and exaggerated claims.

Activities

Give each child a copy of sheet **17a**. Ask them to read the adverts. Which adverts do they find the most eye-catching? Why? What do we learn about each product? What does each advert say is especially good about the product? Would any of these adverts encourage them to buy? Bear in mind that they are used to explosive, colourful and sometimes violent adverts. Point out that the ones they are looking at would be from magazines or newspapers and not on television.

Ask them if comics contain adverts. How do they compare? Discuss alliteration with the class and point out several examples of it. Ask the children to look at the name of each product. Where do they think the names come from? Do any of the adverts use rhyme?

Ask if the adverts are truthful. Why might they not be? What examples of exaggerated claims can the children find?

Give sheet **17b** to the less able group and sheet **17c** to the more able children and ask them to complete them, giving help where needed. Early finishers might try to write and design an advert of their own.

Plenary

Bring the class together again and hear answers from both groups, encouraging the children to give reasons for their answers. Display any adverts the children may have made. Give the children a chance to discuss their favourite adverts.

Advertising

© May Stevenson

This page may be photocopied for use by the purchasing institution only.

Brilliant Activities for Reading Non-fiction

59

Advertising

Name: ....

1. For each advert, write down words that are close to each other beginning with the same letter:

a)

b)

c)

d)

2. Why is the **DOFO** advert wrong to say **all** dogs?

3. Where do you think they got the name **DOFO** from?

4. Write down any words that rhyme in the **MARKLE** advert:

5. Which advert did you like the most?

6. Which did you like the least?

7. Which advert might make you buy the product?

Advertising

Name: ....

1. Which is your favourite advert from sheet **17a**?

2. Alliteration is used in all the adverts, for example 'Miracle Markle'. Find three other examples of alliteration in the adverts.

a)

b)

c)

3. Where do you think the adverts might not be honest? Why?

4. What important thing do the adverts not mention?

5. How do the adverts grab your attention?

18. Too many words

Aim

The children will read a sentence or paragraph, noting any superfluous words. They will then summarize the text, identifying the most important elements and putting them into bullet points. They will use the bullet points to re-write the text using a limited number of words.

Activities

Have a class discussion about road safety. Ask what they think are important things to remember when crossing a road. Allow as many children as possible to take part in the discussion.

Give sheet **18a** to the children and ask them to read the text. Are there any words that appear more than once in the sentence? Are they all necessary? Are there other words or phrases that could be left out? Ask the children to underline the main points in the sentence and fill in the three boxes on the sheet. More able children can also complete sheet **18b** afterwards. Give help where needed.

Ask the children to write a summary of the passage on sheet **18a**.

Plenary

Ask as many children as possible to read out their answers and discuss where necessary. Ask the children to read out their condensed versions of the passage and point out why some of the words in the original sentence did not need to be included.

Too many words

Name: ....

> **To keep yourself safe and to avoid injury to yourself, you should always take great care when crossing a road, by remembering to look carefully both ways and also by remembering to listen in case something is coming which you cannot see properly because of parked cars.**

The passage above gives some good advice but it has far too many words in it. Read it carefully, decide which are the most important points in it and underline them. Then re-write these points below, using as few words as you can:

1.
2.
3.

Too many words

Name: ....

Some things are important to remember if you want to be healthy. You should try to avoid eating too many things like pastries, cakes, sweets and greasy food like chips, burgers, sausage rolls and crisps. Fruit, vegetables, salad, rice, pasta and whole grain foods are delicious and very good for you. Porridge is excellent too. You should not drink too many fizzy drinks, and you must clean you teeth regularly and replace your toothbrush when it is old and the bristles are bent, because then it does not clean your teeth efficiently.

1. This passage has too many words in it! Choose the most important points and use them to fill in the table below:

Food that is good for me	
Food that is not so good for me	
Other advice	

2. Now re-write the main points from the passage in fewer words. Use the back of this sheet.

19. Reporting

Aim

The children will discuss different kinds of reports and read some examples. They will recognize the reports' purpose, how they begin in order to orientate the reader, their chronological sequence, the degree of formality and how detailed they are.

Activities

Have a class discussion about reports in general. Where might the children see reports (e.g. sports reports in newspapers, letters to parents from school or private reports like diaries)? Why do people write these reports? Do any of the children keep a diary? Can they think of any famous diaries (e.g. Anne Frank, Samuel Pepys)? Try to involve as many children as possible in the discussion.

Divide the class into two groups according to ability. Give the less able children sheet **19a** and the more able children sheet **19b**. Talk the less able children through their sheet and help any children who need it. After completing the first sheet, the more able children can proceed to sheet **19c**.

Plenary

Bring the class together again and ask where else they might find reports and why. Go over the answers to sheets **19a**, **19b** and **19c**. Look at how each report begins. How do they let the reader know what the report will be about? Ask which reports are formal and which are informal. Discuss the degree of detail in each report. Why do they not include unnecessary information?

Extension activity

If time allows, ask the children to write a brief report of what has happened in this lesson.

Reporting

Name: ....

Today, at Corry Football Stadium, Rovers netted a goal in the first ten minutes, from Black. Seekers fought back

with two goals from Stewart. Two minutes into extra time, Jamal lobbed a peach of a ball over the keeper's head, giving Rovers a draw.

1. Write down the first phrase that tells us what the report is going to be about:

   _____

2. How many goals were scored altogether? _____

3. Who scored first? _____

4. Who scored last? _____

5. What does the reporter mean by a "peach of a ball"?

Extension activity
Write a short report of your own about a sports event.

Reporting

Name: ....

Monday	Badminton.
Tuesday	Swimming.
Wednesday	Nothing special.
Thursday	Hair cut.
Friday	Mandy came round and we dressed up, put on make-up and sang. Great fun!
Saturday	Hockey (lost!). Cinema – good film.
Sunday	Finished homework – took ages.

1. Where do you think you might find this information?

2. Who has written it?

3. Is the writer old or young?

4. Which was the best day?

5. Who is the writer's friend?

6. Does the report mention everything that happened each day? Why?

7. Who is meant to read this information?

8. Why do you think it was written?

Extension activity

Write your own diary extract for a week.

Reporting

Name: ....

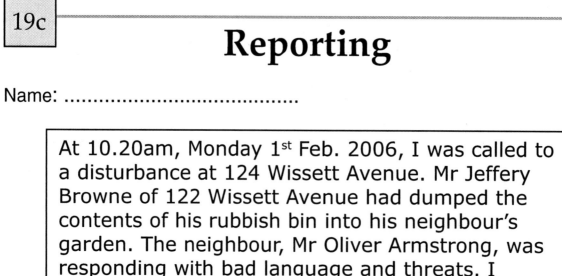

At 10.20am, Monday 1st Feb. 2006, I was called to a disturbance at 124 Wissett Avenue. Mr Jeffery Browne of 122 Wissett Avenue had dumped the contents of his rubbish bin into his neighbour's garden. The neighbour, Mr Oliver Armstrong, was responding with bad language and threats. I talked to the two men and they both calmed down. Mr Browne apologized and removed the rubbish. Mr Armstrong agreed to stop parking his car in front of Mr Browne's gate.

1. Who might write a report like this?

2. How do we know exactly when and where the incident took place?

3. What do you think caused the incident?

4. Why do you think police officers have to report things so carefully?

Extension activity
Write your own police report about a similar incident.

---

20. Breakfast made easy

Aim

The children will read and evaluate a recipe, discussing its purpose. They will consider the organization and layout of a recipe and assess its clarity and usefulness.

Activities

This exercise lends itself to working in groups of mixed ability. Ask the children to read the instructions on sheet **20a** in their group and discuss them. What kind of instructions are they? Who might they be written for?

The children should then work on their own, reading the instructions again and answering the questions.

Discuss the layout of recipes. What do you need in a recipe to make it easy to follow? Ask the children to try to write simple instructions of their own, making them as clear as possible. These could be for any task, such as washing the car, tidying a bedroom, shopping, etc. Ask them to exchange their instructions with a friend and read each other's.

Plenary

Go over the worksheet with the children, hearing as many of their answers as possible. Do they think the recipe for making scrambled eggs is clear enough? Then ask to hear the instructions they have written for each other, and discuss how easy they think these are to follow. What is the purpose of the instructions? How well laid out are they? How clear are they?

Breakfast made easy

Name: ....

You must ask permission if you want to try this at home!

Scrambled eggs

Ingredients
large knob of butter
2 eggs
2 tablespoons of milk
salt and pepper
buttered toast

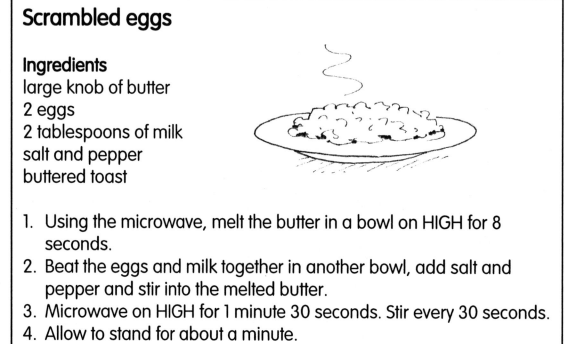

1. Using the microwave, melt the butter in a bowl on HIGH for 8 seconds.
2. Beat the eggs and milk together in another bowl, add salt and pepper and stir into the melted butter.
3. Microwave on HIGH for 1 minute 30 seconds. Stir every 30 seconds.
4. Allow to stand for about a minute.
5. Serve on hot buttered toast.

1. Do you think these instructions are easy to follow? Why?

2. When would these instructions be useless?

3. Using these instructions do you think you would be well organized, or in a muddle?

21. The holiday

Aim

The children will consider the purpose of note-taking and how this affects the nature of the notes made.

Activities

As a whole class discuss note-taking. When and why do we do it? Ask for examples, such as shopping lists, football fixtures, Christmas lists, homework, etc. Why do we not write these notes in whole sentences and paragraphs?

Hand out sheet **21a** to the less able children and sheet **21b** to the more able. Read the text on sheet **21b** with the children and discuss it. Ask them to complete the worksheets. Give help where needed.

Plenary

As a whole class hear the answers to both sheets and discuss why it was important for these children to take notes and how they had to concentrate on what their parents would need to know about the holiday. Discuss further any other cases when the children might need to take notes, and what kind of notes would be appropriate. Discuss the difference between lists and bullet points.

The holiday

Name: ....

A class of children was told to take notes while their teacher told them this:

> "We are going to the Lake District in June of next year. You will need equipment for water sports, hill walking or painting, depending on which you choose. You will also need a sleeping bag, pillow cases and towels. Every five children will be supervised by one adult. The cost will be around £250 each. You can pay in instalments."

1. Where is the school trip going to?

2. How much will it cost?

3. What can I do if I don't have the money right now?

The holiday

Name: ....

A class of children was told to take notes while their teacher told them the following information:

> "Your parents will receive a letter later but here is some news in advance. We are going to the Lake District in June of next year. You will need equipment for water sports, hill walking or painting, depending on which activities you choose. You will also need a sleeping bag, pillow cases and towels. Every five children will be supervised by one adult. The cost will be around £250 each. Your parents can pay in instalments."

1. Here are some questions from parents. Try to answer them:

a) Where is the school trip going to?

b) How much will it cost?

c) How many adults will be supervising the children?

d) What can I do if I don't have the money right now?

e) What will my child need to take?

2. Why was it important for the children to take notes?

22. Little Red Riding Hood

Aim

The children will read a story for enjoyment and note the use of speech marks. They will make notes on the important points so that they can re-tell the story orally.

Activities

With the whole class, ask the children to take turns at reading sections of "Little Red Riding Hood" on sheet **22a**. Allow the children to discuss the story at length.

Go over sheet **22b** with the less able children and ask them to complete it. Remind them of the speech marks needed around the spoken words. Give help where required.

Give sheet **22c** to the more able pupils and ask them to complete it.

Plenary

Bring the class together again. Ask the less able pupils to re-tell the dialogue section of the story using what they have written on their sheets. Then ask some of the more able children to re-tell the whole story using only the notes they made on their sheets.

Little Red Riding Hood

Once upon a time a little girl called Little Red Riding Hood (because she wore a red coat with a hood) lived in a forest with her mother and father. Her father was a woodcutter who chopped down trees with a huge axe.

Little Red Riding Hood's grandmother lived deep in the forest and one day the little girl went to visit her and took a basket of food. On the way, Little Red Riding Hood met a wolf who tried to make friends with her. When she told the wolf where she was going it ran away. She did not know that it would run ahead of her and swallow up her grandmother!

When Little Red Riding Hood arrived at her grandmother's house she saw who she thought was her grandmother lying in bed.

"Why, Grandmother, what big ears you have!" she said.

"All the better to hear you with," the wolf replied.

"Why, Grandmother, what big eyes you have!" she said.

"All the better to see you with," the wolf replied.

"Why, Grandmother, what big teeth you have!" she said.

"All the better to EAT you with!" snarled the wolf and leapt out of bed.

Little Red Riding Hood screamed and ran from the cottage. Luckily her father was working nearby and when he saw the wolf he swung his axe and chopped it in half. Out stepped Grandmother quite unharmed.

Little Red Riding Hood never walked alone in the forest again.

© May Stevenson

Brilliant Activities for Reading Non-fiction

Little Red Riding Hood

Name: ....

1. Fill in the missing speech from the story. How does the wolf reply to Little Red Riding Hood?

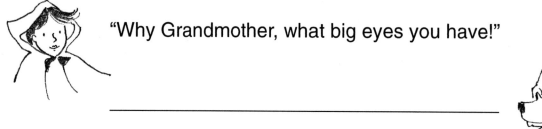

"Why Grandmother, what big ears you have!"

_____

_____

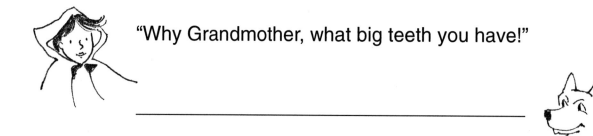

"Why Grandmother, what big eyes you have!"

_____

_____

"Why Grandmother, what big teeth you have!"

_____

_____

2. What does the wolf do next?

Little Red Riding Hood

Name: ....

You may be asked to tell the story of Little Red Riding Hood to the class. You will only be allowed notes to help you. Make notes from each section of the story in the table below, including all the important points.

Title of story: _____

What happens first?
What happens next?
Then what happens?
How does it end?

23. Houses for sale

Aim

The children will read some advertisements and locate information confidently and efficiently by skimming to gain the overall sense of the text, and then scanning to find specific information. They will also discuss when it is appropriate to use these techniques.

Activities

Give the children sheet **23a** and ask them to quickly read the paragraph about the first property once. Then ask them to turn the sheet over and write down on the back as much of it as they can remember. Do the same with the other two paragraphs.

Discuss their answers, letting them check if they missed anything. Stress that this is 'skimming' and that it is likely that they will forget things. Read the description of skimming at the top of the sheet together.

Give out sheet **23b** and explain that now the children will be 'scanning'. Ask the more able pupils to complete the sheet. Read over everything with the less able children until they are confident and let them fill in the answers.

Plenary

Working as a class, ask for the children's answers to sheet **23b** and discuss different options. Ask the children if they can remember the difference between skimming and scanning. Why is skimming useful when you are looking at houses for sale? Why would it be important to read the text more closely if you were interested in one of the houses? Can the children think of other times when you would need to skim or scan text?

Houses for sale

Skimming is reading quickly, trying to pick up information without reading every single word.

Below are three descriptions of different properties that are for sale. Skim the information, then turn the sheet over and write down as much as you can remember.

NEW PROPERTIES ADDED EVERY WEEK

Gloucester Street: Fourth floor flat (no lift), two bedrooms, bathroom with shower, kitchen, lounge, small dining room, balcony, good view.

Wilson Avenue: Semi-detached bungalow, lounge, dining room, three bedrooms, loft room, bathroom, shower room, garage, large garden, quiet street, close to schools.

REDUCED PRICE

Parkington Crescent: Ground floor flat, quiet area, living room, one bedroom, bathroom with shower, small, easily kept garden, close to shops and public transport.

NEW

Houses for sale

Name: ....

Now answer these questions. You will need to refer to the text on sheet **23a** again, this time reading it more slowly and carefully to find the answers. This is called **scanning**.

1. Which house would be the most suitable for a family with young children? Why?

2. Which would be the most suitable for an elderly person? Why?

3. Which would be the most suitable for a fit young couple? Why?

4. Which house might not be suitable for a person living alone? Why?

24. The new hall

Aim
The children will read some advertisements and locate information confidently and efficiently by skimming to gain the overall sense of the text, and then scanning to find specific information. They will also discuss when it is appropriate to use these techniques.

Activities
Hand out sheet **24a** and ask the whole class to read the text. Give the children five minutes to complete the questions, working in pairs.

Give the less able children sheet **24b**. Re-read the passage with them and then ask them to fill in the gaps, with help if needed.

Give the more able children sheet **24c** and a page each from a mail order catalogue showing toys, clothes, etc., and ask them to complete the task.

Plenary
Gather the children together and discuss the answers to both sheets. Ask when else they might skim a text and when they would need to scan, e.g. telephone directories, internet, lists, timetables, etc.

The new hall

Name: ....

Read this report quickly so that you take in the main ideas:

The new village hall has a wooden floor suitable for games or dancing. Markings will be made for five-a-side football and netball.

There is a fine stage and a piano for entertainment of all kinds.

High quality curtains can be closed to darken the room. There are ladies and gents' toilets, and a small kitchen for tea making.

There are three steps up to the entrance and there is also a door on the side with a ramp for disabled people.

Now answer these questions. You will need to read the text more slowly and carefully to find the answers.

1. Are there toilets in the hall?

2. Is there a kitchen?

3. What is the hall floor suitable for? Name as many things as you can.

4. What provision is there for disabled people?

5. When and why would the curtains be drawn?

The new hall

Name: ....

Read the passage on sheet **24a** again, then turn it over. Try to remember and fill in the words that are missing in the blank spaces on this sheet. Don't look at the other sheet!

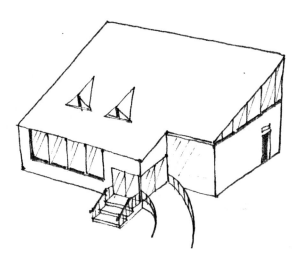

The new village ....

has a .... floor

suitable for games or

.... Markings will

be .... for five-a-side

.... and netball.

There is a fine stage and a .... for entertainment of all

kinds.

High quality .... can be closed to darken the room.

There are ladies and gents' .... , and a small kitchen for

tea making.

There are three .... up to the entrance and there is also a

door on the side with a .... for disabled people.

Scanning challenge

Name: ....

You will need a page taken from a mail order catalogue.

Skim the page and make up some questions about various products. For example, you could ask about the price of something, or about who it is suitable for.

Swap your questions and your page with a friend's. Scan their page to find the answers to the questions.

1. _____

2. _____

3. _____

4. _____

5. _____

6. _____

25. Letters to the editor

Aim

The children will read, compare and evaluate extracts from letters written to the editors of newspapers or magazines. They will discuss the purpose of each letter and look for facts and opinions. They will understand characteristics of persuasive language.

Activities

If possible, have some letters from a newspaper or magazine to read to the children and discuss.

Hand out sheet **25a** and ask all of the children to read the extracts from letters written to editors. What is each letter about? What is the main point they are trying to make? What other subjects might people write about to an editor?

Discuss with the children which extracts tell us facts and which contain opinions. Do any of them give an opinion as if it were a fact? Do any of them include exaggeration? For example, in the first letter, is it really true that fireworks frighten all pets and all old people?

Which extracts complain about something? Which try to persuade the reader about something? Do any of them contain language that makes them more memorable, such as alliteration?

Ask the less able children to complete sheet **25b**. Give help and encouragement where needed. The more able children should be asked to complete sheet **25c**. Make a list on the board of things the children might want to write about and discuss how they would begin a letter to an editor.

Plenary

Ask the pupils who have done sheet **25b** to read out their letters. Then go over the results of sheet **25c**, with the less able children listening to the results and giving their opinions orally if possible.

Letters to the editor

Here are some extracts from letters written to the editors of newspapers or magazines:

A **Ban Fireworks!**
Fireworks going off for weeks on end frighten pets and old people. I think fireworks should be banned except for November 5ᵗʰ.

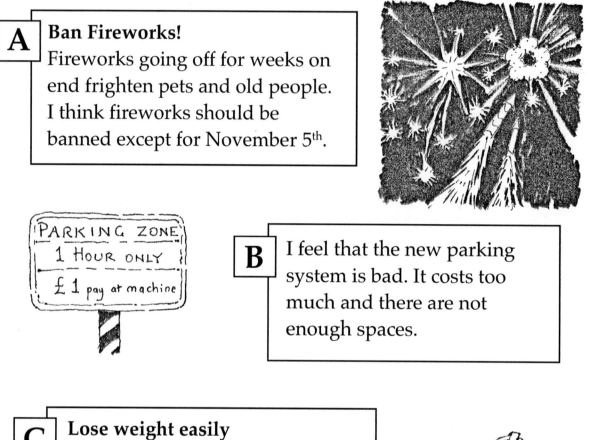

B I feel that the new parking system is bad. It costs too much and there are not enough spaces.

C **Lose weight easily**
Walking in the park or country-side helps you to lose weight. It also helps you sleep at night. Forget about T.V. or videos. *Walking* is better than *watching*!

D A new bus time-table is coming into use next week. It is available from the central bus station.

Letters to the editor

Name: ....

Imagine that you have been asked to write a short letter for your school magazine giving your opinion on one of the subjects below.

1. Choose a subject and then write your letter in the box below:

My favourite pop group   **Things I hate doing**

My best friend   **The best film I have seen**

2. Why did you choose to write about that subject?

Letters to the editor

Name: ....

1. Read the letters on sheet **25a** and then fill in the table below by ticking what each letter does:

LETTER	Gives information	Gives an opinion	Persuades the reader about something	Complains
A				
B				
C				
D				

2. Write a brief letter to a newspaper or magazine, complaining about something:

26. The flyer

Aim
The children will read and comment on various newspaper headlines, adverts and flyers. They will consider whether the flyers are factual or not, and look at persuasive writing. They will note the deliberate use of exaggeration and ambiguity and understand how opinion can be disguised as fact.

Activities
Have some glaring newspaper headlines and some adverts for the children to look at. Make sure that the content matches your pupils' maturity! Discuss these with the whole class, looking at how they attract the reader's attention. Do they tell us facts? Do they exaggerate anything?

Read the two flyers on sheets **26a** and **26b** with the children. After discussing the flyers divide the children into two groups by ability. The less able children should read sheet **26a** again with the teacher and then attempt the questions. Give help where needed. The more able children should tackle sheet **26b**. (The more able children will need a copy of both sheets to answer the last question.)

Plenary
As a class, discuss the answers to all of the questions. What facts do the adverts tell us? How do they persuade the reader to buy the product? Do the children think the flyers are dishonest?

If there is time, ask the children to write adverts of their own and display them.

Extension activity
Ask the children to be on the lookout for more examples of flyers like these and to bring them in. Discuss these as a class, focusing on persuasive language.

The flyer

Name: ....

Here is a flyer which might be posted through your door:

Dancing made easy...

This just might be the easiest way in the world to *learn to dance*! We are convinced that if you use our product properly, in a very short time you will be able to *dance like a champion*.

For more details, call: 01962 451234

1. Do you think some people would phone this number? Why?

2. What does the flyer not tell you?

3. Why are some parts of the flyer in big, bold letters?

4. If you bought the product but still could not dance, how could the advertisers get away with the things they say?

5. If you bought the product and found it did not work, why might you not want to complain?

The flyer

Name: ....

Here is a flyer which might be posted through your door:

Food for thought

We've all heard the saying:

"You are what you eat"

So why not try our wonderful new product? We are confident that you will **feel better**, **look better**, **think better** and probably **live longer** as a result.

Just two capsules a day could change your life!

Phone this number for details: 07326 774129

---

1. What claims does this flyer make?

2. What does the flyer not tell you?

3. Why might they not tell you some things?

4. If you used the product and felt no different, why might you not want to complain?

5. Make a list of the words in both leaflets that help the advertisers to get away with the claims they make.

27. Persuasive words and phrases

Aim

The children will read various adverts and look for persuasive words and phrases. They will consider the use of ambiguous language and discuss how honest and effective the adverts are.

Activities

Have a few adverts ready to display. Ask the children to choose their favourite. What is it about them that makes people buy? Discuss with the whole class at length, writing the persuasive words and phrases from the adverts on the board.

Go over sheet **27a** with the less able children, discussing it at length, and help them to answer sheet **27b**. Ask the more able children to read sheet **27c** and then tackle the questions on sheet **27d**.

Plenary

Read over sheets **27b** and **27d** with the whole class and take as many of the children's answers as possible.

Do the children think that adverts are good things? Why?

Extension activity

Ask the children to make up an advert of their own. Read them out and discuss.

Newspapers, magazines, comics and adverts often use specially chosen words or phrases to persuade us to buy things, or to believe things. Here are a few examples:

A

Nobody can resist a *Candy Cake*!

B

She's the loveliest girl in the world.

C

Possibly the best furniture you will ever buy.

D

Professional footballers won't kick anything else.

Persuasive words and phrases

Name: ....

Look at the adverts on sheet **27a** and answer the following questions:

Advert A

Would this make you want to buy a "Candy Cake"? Why? Is the advert telling the truth?

Advert B

Could this claim be true? Why?

Advert C

Why do they say "possibly"? Would you still want to buy their furniture?

Advert D

Why might this make you want to buy the football? Is it telling the truth?

Persuasive words and phrases

Newspapers, magazines, comics and adverts often use specially chosen words or phrases to persuade us to buy things, or to believe things. Here are a few examples:

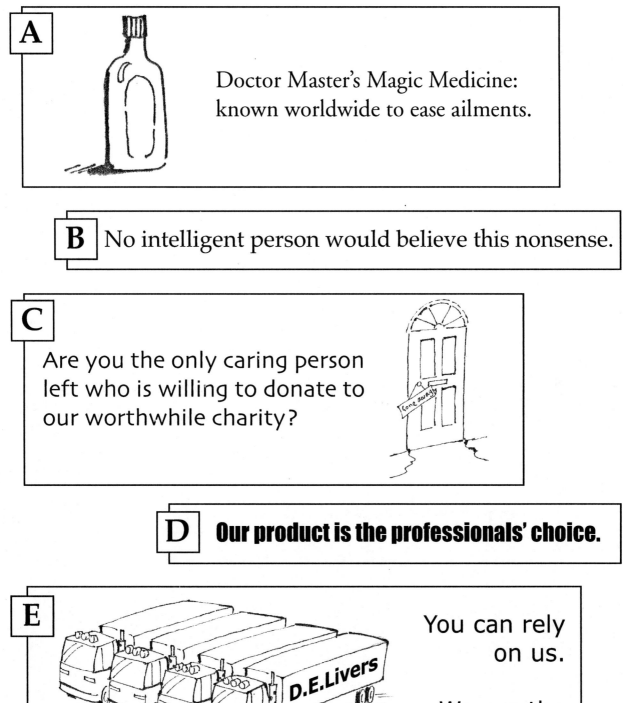

A Doctor Master's Magic Medicine: known worldwide to ease ailments.

B No intelligent person would believe this nonsense.

C Are you the only caring person left who is willing to donate to our worthwhile charity?

D Our product is the professionals' choice.

E D.E.Livers

You can rely on us.

We are the best.

Persuasive words and phrases

Name: ....

Look at the adverts on sheet **27c** and answer the following questions:

Advert A
Why might this persuade you to buy the medicine? Is it telling the truth? Why?

Advert B
Why might this statement make you think something is not true?

Advert C
Why might this make you donate to the charity?

Advert D
Why might this claim not be true?

Advert E
Would you believe this statement? Why?

28. My pop star life

Aim

The children will read extracts from a biography and an autobiography, and distinguish between the two. They will recognize the difference between the first and third person voice. They will distinguish between fact, fiction and opinion, and understand the difference between explicit and implicit points of view. They will assess the reliability of the biographical and autobiographical accounts in the light of these factors.

Activities

As a class, read the two accounts of Boulder Dam's life on sheets **28a** and **28b** and discuss them. What differences can they find between the two versions? Which version do the children believe? Why?

Discuss the meaning of 'biography' and 'autobiography'. Ask the children who is speaking in each of the extracts. Explain the difference between the first and third person voice, giving other examples. Ask if any of the children possess a biography of a pop star or footballer and what they think of that person.

Remind the children of the difference between fact, fiction and opinion, and ask them for some examples. Explain that an opinion can be very obvious, and this is called an explicit point of view. However, sometimes it is not clear straight away that the writer is stating an opinion, as it is only hinted at, and this is called an implicit point of view. Give examples of both.

Distribute sheet **28c** to the less able pupils and sheet **28d** to the more able. Give help where needed.

Plenary

As a class, discuss the children's answers to both sheets. Ask each of them to write down an example of a fact, fiction, and an opinion and discuss them as a class.

Extension activity

The children could write about someone they would like to be in the style of an autobiographical account.

My pop star life

On a Roll: My Story

by Boulder Dam

I was born in a poor area of Liverpool. It was a noisy, crowded place for a child to grow up in. My dad was a sailor and was lost at sea off Africa. My mam and I had very little to live on and the poverty all around me made me determined to be rich.

Although I had no training in music, I taught myself to play on an old, second-hand guitar. I also wrote my own songs and trudged round all the record companies and agents looking for a start. It was exhausting and my mam wanted me to give up and try to get a job with a local builder.

None of the record labels or agencies wanted me, so I had no choice but to start working as a builder.

However, at long last I manage to join a small band. At weekends I played lead guitar with them, and during the week I did building work.

I worked very hard and eventually formed my own group, "The Boulders". I called it that because playing the guitar was much better than shifting boulders on a building site. Little did I know back then how famous "The Boulders" would eventually become.

My pop star life

"Boulder Dam"
The Life of Joe Markham
by Bill Walker

The famous pop star "Boulder Dam" was born on 3rd March 1967 as Joe Markham, to parents Mary and Dan Markham. They lived in a large, new house just outside Liverpool. It was a pleasant place for young Joe to grow up in. His father owned a big shop and Joe often helped him to deliver groceries to the neighbours.

The boy was also fond of music and so his father bought him a good guitar. After many expensive lessons, when Joe was able to play well, his dad arranged for him to perform alongside a group who were playing at a local hall.

Most of the neighbours came to support the boy and the group's leader was so impressed that he gave Joe a place in the band. Joe chose the stage name of "Boulder Dam". He had remembered this name from a geography lesson in which he learned that "Hoover Dam" in America was originally called "Boulder Dam". Joe also liked the name because he thought it sounded big and strong.

After a few years, Joe's dad gave him the money to set up his own group, "The Boulders", and it was with them that Joe would later win fame and fortune.

My pop star life

Name: ....

1. Which account do you think is true?

2. Why might a pop star want to make up a story?

3. Why do you think he changed his name?

4. Write down one **fact** about "Boulder Dam".

5. Write down something that you think is **fiction**.

My pop star life

Name: ....

A **biography** is an account about someone's life, written by another person.
An **autobiography** is an account about someone's life, written by that person.

Explicit means something that is stated clearly.
Implicit means something that is hinted at.

1. Which of these passages is a biography and which an autobiography?

2. "It was a noisy, crowded place" is an **explicit** point of view about the area. What does it tell you about the area Joe says he grew up in?

3. "A big shop" contains an **implicit** comment about Joe's lifestyle. What kind of lifestyle does this suggest that Joe had when he was growing up?

4. Write one thing from either passage which you think is a **fact**.

5. Write one thing from either passage which you think is **fiction**.

6. Write one thing from either passage which you think is an **opinion**.

Extension activity
Write a short autobiography for yourself.

29. Sports reports

Aim

The children will read two reports and comment critically on their language, style and success. They will look for examples of metaphors and note the effect that these create. They will see how reports can be objective or subjective.

Activities

Give each child a copy of sheet **29a**. Ask them to read it for themselves and to carefully study the football match report. Ask them to look for words which are used for effect but which are not literally true, such as "explosive". How many examples of this can they find? Discuss the two reports and ask some children to point out the differences between them. Which team do they think the writer of the football report supports? Why? Do they think the writer of the second report supports any individual cyclist in particular? Why? Why do the children think such reports are published?

Give each child a copy of sheet **29b** and ask them to complete it. If there is time, they could write a sports report of their own.

Give help to the less able children by reading the reports again with them, discussing them and talking them through the question sheet if necessary.

Plenary

Discuss the pupils' answers and hear any of their sports reports, asking for opinions of them from the class. Where might they find such reports? Ask them to look for similar reports at home and, if possible, to bring them in for display.

Sports reports

Below is a report of a football match:

After an explosive start, the visitors looked like they would stay in the driving seat and wrap up a win. In the second half however, Tamir and Johnson from the home team came alive and poached two sweet goals to grab control of the game. This drained the opposition's confidence and unlocked a cracking victory.

The home coach was delighted with the result and promised both Tamir and Johnson a place in the team for the next match, and the chance of a permanent place if they played as well as this again.

The coach of the visiting team was less than happy and was heard leaving the pitch muttering, "Changes needed... Some players must go!"

Here is a report from a cycling club:

Bill Thomas of Raeburn Club has become cyclist of the year after winning every race and gaining 40 points. This is a remarkable achievement considering the difficulty of the rides and the appalling weather conditions during some of the races.

Bill took the lead early in almost every race and managed to hold it, despite Ken Drake often being very close behind him. Ken should be congratulated for his determination in keeping up with Bill's high standard and almost catching him several times.

Praise also goes to new rider Harry O'Neil, who won a creditable 19 points.

Sports reports

Name: ....

1. Which of the two sports reports did you find more interesting? Why do you think this is?

2. In the football report some words are used in an unusual way, e.g. "explosive start" (nothing actually exploded!). Write down as many other examples of words like this as you can.

3. Why do you think this kind of writing is used in sports reports?

4. What pieces of information were missing in the cycling club report?

Extension activity
Write a report of your own (about any sport) and make it as interesting and exciting as possible.

30. Granton School football club

Aim

The children will read a non-chronological report and discuss its content and language. They will look at how the introduction orientates the reader, how facts are expressed, the use of generalizations, the tense, and informative and impersonal language.

Activities

Give each child a copy of sheet **30a**. Let the children take turns at reading parts of the report aloud, to ensure that all the children have understood it.

Discuss the report with the children and ask them to comment on it. Why was it written? Does it go into detail or give an overview? What do we learn from the first paragraph? What facts can the children find in the text? What tense is the report written in?

Give sheet **30b** to the less able children and talk them through it before asking them to complete it. Give sheet **30c** to the more able children and ask them to complete it. Give help where needed in the class.

Plenary

Bring the children together and discuss their answers. Ask why they think the girls' changing rooms are still adequate. Is it because there are more boys than girls in the school or because fewer girls are interested in football? Discuss. Why does the report not give the result of every game? Do the children think the report has been written primarily to inform or to persuade? Discuss the use of informative and impersonal language. Encourage dialogue amongst the children.

Granton School football club

Granton School Football Club

End of season report to parents

The club meets every Monday after school. It begins by listing the results of the various teams in the past week, before going on to the warm-up, training and practice games.

The boys' changing rooms have now been extended. The girls' changing rooms cope adequately at present.

The success rate of our football teams is high, but it is not all about winning. Keeping fit, making friends and travelling to meet other students is all part of being in the club.

We are always in need of money to pay for football strips, equipment and travelling expenses.

We would welcome your help in fund-raising and thank you for all the tremendous support you have given to us in the past.

Granton School football club

Name: ....

1. What does the first line of the report tell parents?

2. What three things do the children gain from being in the club?

a) Keeping _____

b) Making _____

c) Travelling to meet _____

3. The club always needs money to pay for what three things?

a) Football _____

b) _____

c) Travelling _____

4. What does the club want parents to do?

Granton School football club

Name: ....

1. What does the first line of the report tell parents?

2. Are there any girls in the football club?

3. Do the teams win many matches? Which words tell us this?

4. What three things do the children gain from being in the club?

5. Does the report tell us about the success of any one team?

6. Why do you think this is?

7. What does the club want parents to do?

Extension activity
Make up your own report telling parents about another after school club.

31. School uniform

Aim

The children will read two opposing points of view and look at how the arguments are constructed using persuasive language. They will discuss the use of fact and opinion, and how points are expressed and linked. They will recognize the use of examples and evidence, and how the writer pre-empts and answers potential objections and appeals to the known views and feelings of the reader. They will decide how effective these arguments are.

Activities

Ask the children to think about compulsary full school uniform. Do they like it? Or, if they do not have to wear it, would they like to? What are the advantages and disadvantages? Encourage as much dialogue as possible. If they could choose whether or not to wear a uniform, would they wear it?

Hand out sheet **31a**, read it through with the class. Discuss whether the text is about facts or opinions, and look at opinions expressed as fact. Does Kailey give examples or evidence to support her argument? Ask the children why she talks about what "some people think" in the fourth point.

Give the less able children sheet **31c** and ask them to fill in the answers. Give help if needed. Give the more able children sheets **31b** and **31d**, and ask them to answer the questions.

Plenary

Gather the children together and discuss as many of their answers and opinions as possible. Ask them why Ryan says "if you are proud of your school" in his last point, and discuss how he appeals to the reader's feelings to support his argument. Discuss the rhetorical question in his fifth point, asking the children how Ryan expects the reader to answer.

Do the children think these arguments are effective? Who do they think argues their point of view better?

Extension activity

Write a persuasive letter to your headteacher asking him or her to ban school uniform. Give reasons for your opinion.

School uniform

Kailey's point of view:

1. I don't like wearing school uniform because it is dull and boring.

2. School uniform is expensive, especially for families with several children.

3. If uniform wasn't necessary, then people could buy cheaper clothes.

4. Some people say that not wearing uniforms could lead to trouble because vandals couldn't be traced, but people in school uniform can cause trouble too.

5. I feel that if I were allowed to wear what I liked I would be happier and concentrate on my work more. I think that we should be allowed to choose whether we wear school uniform or our own clothes.

School uniform

Ryan's point of view:

1. I like wearing school uniform. I don't have to wonder each morning what I'm going to wear, and it is warm and comfortable.

2. Police officers wear uniforms so that we know who they are. We are school children and our uniform tells people that.

3. If we didn't have a uniform, some people might wear very expensive clothes and others would feel bad because they couldn't afford to.

4. Some people might say that a uniform is boring, but they have every evening and all weekend to wear what they like.

5. Would you concentrate on your school work if you were fussing about clothes and feeling down because you couldn't afford different clothes for each day?

6. If you are proud of your school you should be proud to wear its uniform.

School uniform

Name: ....

Kailey's point of view:

1. What is Kailey's first reason for not liking school uniform?

2. Read reasons 2 and 3 and explain why school uniform is not always good for people with several children.

3. Why do you think people might not cause trouble if they are in uniform?

4. If you had to decide whether your school made pupils wear school uniform or not, what would you decide? Why?

School uniform

Name: ....

Kailey's point of view:

1. What is Kailey's first reason for not liking school uniform?

2. Read reasons 2 and 3 and explain why school uniform is not always good for people with several children.

3. Why do you think people might not cause trouble if they are in uniform?

Ryan's point of view:

4. What three reasons does Ryan give for wanting to wear a uniform?

5. What is Ryan's last reason for wearing a uniform?

6. Why might you feel bad if some people chose not to wear a uniform?

7. Why does Ryan not agree that wearing a uniform is boring?

8. Write down as many examples of people who wear a uniform as you can think of.

9. If you had to decide whether your school made pupils wear school uniform or not, what would you decide? Why?

32. Staying out late at night

Aim

The children will read two opposing points of view and discuss the features of balanced written arguments and persuasive language. They will see how the different sides of the argument are summarized using facts to support them, and how personal opinions are expressed.

Activities

Read over both sections of sheet **32a** with the whole class, pointing out that the pupil involved could be either a girl or a boy, and that the issues apply equally to both sexes. Ask for opinions. Encourage lots of discussion.

Give the less able children sheet **32b** and go over the sheet orally before asking them to complete it. Give the more able children sheet **32c** to complete. Give help and encouragement where needed.

Plenary

Bring the class together again and hear the children's answers to both sheets. Discuss the difference between fact and opinion and ask for examples.

Point out "nearly thirteen" and "only twelve". Who is right? When might people say things like this? Encourage discussion.

Staying out late at night

Alex says:

"I'm nearly thirteen and Mum wants me home by 8.30 on a Friday evening. Most youth clubs don't finish until 8 o'clock. After the club, I have no time to chat with my mates who don't go home until 9.30. I could lose friends and be lonely in school. It is perfectly safe at that time of night. I feel that my mum doesn't trust me."

Alex's mum says:

"8.30pm seems a fair time to ask Alex to come home on Fridays. After all, she is only twelve, and too young to defend herself if anyone tried to attack her. If her friends are true friends, they will still like her even though she has to come home a bit earlier than they do. She has a lot of homework to do and also has to get up early the following morning for her swimming lesson. I love my daughter and want the best for her."

Staying out late at night

Name: ....

1. Write down one reason that Alex gives for staying out later than 8.30pm.

2. Write down one reason that Alex's mum gives for her to come home by 8.30pm.

3. What age does Alex say she is?

4. What ages does her mum say Alex is?

5. Who do you think is right about whether Alex should be allowed to stay out late? Why?

Staying out late at night

Name: ....

1. Write down three things that Alex says in favour of staying out later than 8.30pm.

a)

b)

c)

2. Write down three things that Alex's mum says about why she should come home at 8.30pm.

a)

b)

c)

3. Write down a personal opinion of Alex's.

4. Write down a personal opinion of her mum's.

5. What is your opinion? Why?

Brilliant Activities for Reading Non-fiction

33. Putting it bluntly

Aim

The children will read examples of warning letters and identify the key features of informal and impersonal formal language, and look at different ways of expressing the same concept. They will discuss the present tense and the passive voice, and when and why these are used.

Activities

Read sheets **33a** and **33b** with all the children and discuss the letters at length. Look at the differences in language and style. Which is more friendly? Which is more threatening? Are they formal or informal? How do we know? What tense is used? Look at how the first letter uses the passive voice and discuss the effect this has.

Read the letters on sheet **33c** and compare them in a similar way. Ask the less able children to complete sheet **33d**, giving help where needed. Ask the more able children to tackle the questions on sheet **33e**, using sheets **33a** and **33b**.

Plenary

Discuss the answers to both sheets and ask the children when they might receive formal letters, such as notice of dental appointments, letters from the Headteacher, etc. Write a list on the board.

Putting it bluntly

Riverston & Co.
Chalney Street
Hempstead
HP29 2RU

24th September 2005

Dear Mr Tilby,

It has come to our attention that the amount owing in your account with our company now exceeds our stipulated limit.

It would benefit our firm greatly if this debt can be cleared or greatly reduced at your earliest convenience.

Yours sincerely,

J Smith

J. Smith
Company Secretary

Putting it bluntly

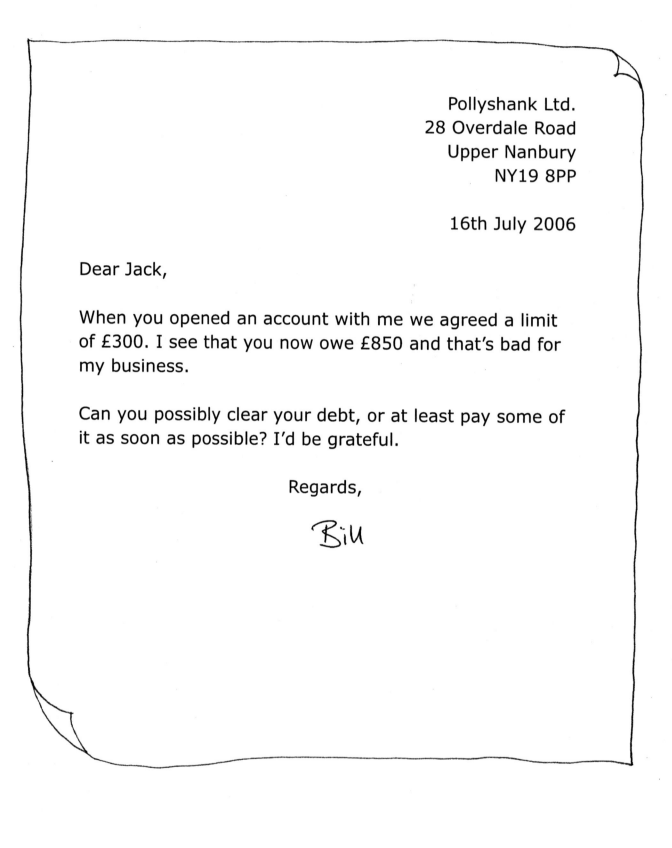

Pollyshank Ltd.
28 Overdale Road
Upper Nanbury
NY19 8PP

16th July 2006

Dear Jack,

When you opened an account with me we agreed a limit of £300. I see that you now owe £850 and that's bad for my business.

Can you possibly clear your debt, or at least pay some of it as soon as possible? I'd be grateful.

Regards,

Bill

Putting it bluntly

Below are two letters sent to workers in different supermarkets:

2nd March 2007

To all staff,

The management team wishes to inform workers that bad time-keeping will not be tolerated.

From now on, late arrivals at work will face instant dismissal.

signed,
A.A. Dawson
Manager

15th October

To all workers on the shop floor,

I've noticed time-keeping hasn't been good recently and this causes a lot of problems to other staff and customers.

Please try to arrive at work on time, otherwise I really regret that I will have to do something about it.

Yours,
Bob Arnold, Manager

Putting it bluntly

Name: ....

Look at the letters on sheet **33c**, and answer the following questions:

1. Which of these letters is formal?

2. When might a boss send a letter like this?

3. The second letter says almost the same thing as the first. What makes it different?

4. What does "tolerated" mean?

5. What does "dismissal" mean?

6. Which manager do you think you would like better?

Putting it bluntly

Name: ....

Look at the letters on sheets **33a** and **33b**, and answer the following questions:

1. Which of these letters is written in formal language?

2. The letters say almost the same thing. What makes them different?

3. Match each phrase from the first letter to the one that means the same thing in the second letter:

Letter 1	Letter 2
a) "It has come to our attention that"	i) "I'd be grateful"
b) "exceeds our stipulated limit"	ii) "Regards"
c) "It would benefit our firm greatly"	iii) "you now owe £850"
d) "at your earliest convenience"	iv) "I see that"
e) "Yours sincerely"	v) "as soon as possible"

4. Which letter is impersonal and which is personal?

5. What does "stipulated limit" mean?

Extension activity
Write a formal reply from Mr. Tilby to the first letter, asking the company for more time to pay what you owe them. Give a reason for this.

34. Crossing the road

Aim

The children will read an article, and then scan it to retrieve information. They will discuss the style and language of the text and evaluate its content.

Activities

Give each child a copy of sheet **34a** and read it with them. Discuss the contents at length, checking that the children understand it and explaining any unfamiliar words. Ask them for their opinions on what they have read and for ideas about how the problem could be tackled. Were they surprised by what the article says? Did they find it interesting? Does it contain facts or opinions? How does the first paragraph help the reader to understand the issue?

The less able children should try to complete sheet **34b**. Ask the more able children to work on sheet **34c**.

Plenary

As a whole class, let some of the less able children read their completed passage on sheet **34b**. Ask for alternative words to fill the gaps with.

Let the more able children read aloud the questions on sheet **34c** and give their answers. Encourage any children who have anything to add to any of the answers to give their opinions.

Extension activity

Children can research the World Health Organization and what it and other organizations are doing to help to reduce road fatalities throughout the world.

Crossing the road

Imagine you are standing by the side of a busy street in New Delhi, India. Dressed in your school uniform, you make the same journey every day on your way to school. But every day, it's just as scary as you try to cross the road, with cars, motorbikes, trucks and other traffic whizzing past you, honking their horns and trying to overtake. At last there's a gap, and you race across, hoping that the oncoming bus has seen you.

Did you know that throughout the world, road accidents are just as deadly as malaria and tuberculosis? Today about 3000 people will lose their lives on roads around the world, including 500 children.

In countries like the United Kingdom less people are killed in crashes than before, because we are all now aware of how things like wearing a seatbelt and obeying the speed limit help to keep us safe. However, in poorer parts of the world the number of people hurt in traffic accidents is going up and up.

The World Health Organization (WHO) has reported that by the year 2020, road accidents will cause at least twice as many deaths each year, unless road safety is improved in developing countries. Poor quality roads, old vehicles and ignoring traffic rules are the main reasons why these countries are so badly affected by this problem.

"This must never happen again," was the conclusion of the coroner after the first ever death in a car accident, in 1896. Today the world faces a huge challenge to reduce the number of people who are killed on the road.

Crossing the road

Name: ....

1. Read the passage below and fill in the missing words:

Road accidents kill and injure a similar number of ....

throughout the world to .... and ....

.... about 3000 people, including 500 .... will be

killed on the road.

In developed .... the number of deaths in traffic accidents

has fallen, but in .... countries it continues to ....

The World Health .... says that there will be at least

.... as many road deaths in 2020, unless action is taken in.

The main causes of crashes in developing countries are poor quality

........................, old vehicles and ignoring .... rules.

After the first ever death in a car accident in ...., the

.... said, "This must never .... again."

2. Did you find the article surprising? Why?

Crossing the road

Name: ....

1. Which two diseases are road traffic fatalities compared to?

2. Find three facts given in the text to show how important the issue of road safety is, especially in developing countries.

   a)

   b)

   c)

3. Why has the number of deaths on the roads decreased in the United Kingdom? Can you think of any other things that drivers and pedestrians should do to keep safe?

4. Why are busy roads often very dangerous in developing countries?

5. What do you think the government in India could do to make the country's roads safer?

6. Pedestrians, cyclists and motorcyclists are the ones who are most at risk on the road. Why do you think this is?

7. How can people throughout the world be made more aware of this issue?

35. Different types of text

Aim

The children will read four short non-fiction texts giving information on different topics. They will discuss their style and characteristics, noting when a writer might choose to write in a given style and form.

Activities

As a class, read the four texts on sheet **35a** and discuss them. How effective are they? What makes them work? Is there anything missing in them that a reader would want to know? Could the style of one be interchanged with another and the text still be effective? Encourage as much dialogue as possible.

Give sheet **35b** to the children. Ask the less able children to complete the first four questions and give help where needed. If they feel able they should be encouraged to try the rest of the sheet. More able children should complete the whole sheet.

Plenary

Go through each question, hearing as many of the children's answers as possible. Ask how they could tell where each text comes from. Ask to hear the short adverts and discuss their effectiveness. Display these.

Different types of text

1 The ear is the organ of the body concerned with hearing and balance. It consists of three parts:

a) **The outer ear**: this collects sound.
b) **The middle ear**: this passes vibrations from the eardrum to the inner ear.
c) **The inner ear**: this has three cavities called the "labyrinth", which help us to balance.

2 **Free-to-view Digital TV PLUS 8 extra channels FREE subscription**
Super sharp picture, ultra-clear sound. No adaptor needed. Delivered, installed and demonstrated **free**.

3 **synonym** *n.* word or phrase identical in meaning to another, or with the same meaning in a particular context. **synonymous** *a.*

4 **After School Club: It's a Must!**

Come along and join the fun! Football, netball or badminton for the sports fans, chess or scrabble for those who prefer something quieter, and pop music at the disco for everybody to dance to.

Make a date for Friday 4pm.

Admission FREE.

Different types of text

Name: ....

1. In what kind of book would you find text 1?

2. Where would you be likely to see text 2?

3. In what kind of book would you find text 3?

4. Where would you be most likely to find text 4?

5. What else could text 1 tell us about the ear?

6. In text 2, what word is used three times? Why do you think this is?

Extension activity
Try writing a short advert of your own for sweets.

Answers to worksheets

Year 3 Term 1

1. Fact or fiction?

Sheet **1a**:
1. fact
2. fact
3. fiction
4. fiction
5. fiction
6. fact

Sheet **1b**:
1. fact
2. fiction
3. fact
4. fiction
5. fact
6. fiction

2. About balloons

Sheet **2a**:
1. lovingly
2. angrily, sly smile
3. *open question*

Sheet **2b**:
1. dictionary or encyclopedia
2. story book
3. lovingly
4. no – angry to have been tied up, happy to be free

3. Finding information

Sheet **3a**:
Food: Batter, Cake, Jelly
Birds: Robin, Sparrow
Clothes: Skirt, Socks, Wellington boots
Forests: Acorns, Robin, Sparrow, Squirrel

Sheet **3b**:
1. Spring
2. Aeroplane
3. Coat
4. Sparrow
5. Sheep
6. Nose
7. Teacher

4. Making faces

Sheet **4a**:
1. raise eyebrows
2. pull eyebrows close together
3. smile
4. frown

Sheet **4b**: *open activity*

Year 3 Term 2

5. Different purposes of writing

Sheet **5a**:
1. cookery book
2. train station
3. for safety
4. *open question*

Sheets **5b** and **5c**: *open questions*

6. Following instructions

Sheet **6a**:
1. protect head if fell off
2. keep warm
3. keep clothes clean

Sheet **6b**:
1. b) if cereal is not poured carefully it will go everywhere
   c) if packet is left open cereal will go soggy
   d) pour milk so it does not splash
   e) if milk is not put back in fridge it will go sour
2. a) 1
   b) 2
   c) 0

Year 3 Term 3

7. Letter writing

Sheet **7b**:
1. letter A
2. letter B
3. sore throat

Sheet **7c**:
1. letter A
2. letter B
3. letter A is formal: has address, full date, 'Dear' and title, then begins with new paragraph
   letter B is informal: only has day, first name, misses out 'Dear', does not start new paragraph
4. Mrs Brown is not friend of Miss Wilson
   Jane is friend of Simone

Sheet **7d**:
1. John is apologizing, asking for wellies back
2. John is school captain
3. formal

8. Understanding what you read

Sheet **8b**:
1. warned to be careful and not go near fireworks
2. he picked a firework up and threw it on the bonfire
3. he was badly burned and taken to hospital
4. *open question*
5. Kevin injured by a firework; warning to children not to play with fireworks, to listen to parents

Sheet **8c**:
1. Jack knocked over by a car outside Silverton park
2. in Lemon Street, by Silverton Park
3. ice-cream van arrived
4. Jack ran across road
5. hit by car
6. taken to hospital
7. busy road runs next to a park
8. *open question*
9. Jack injured by a car; warning to children not to run across road; putting pressure on council improve road safety near park

Answers to worksheets

Year 4 Term 1

9. Fact or opinion?

Sheet **9a**:
1. fact: c,e,h; opinion a,b,d,f,g
2. *open question*

Sheet **9b**:
1. fact: a,e,f; opinion b,c,d
2. *open question*

10. Newspaper headlines

Sheets **10a** and **10b**: *open activities*

11. Painting class

Sheet **11b**:
1. paper, paint, paintbrushes
2. fold paper in half
3. add yellow paint
4. add red paint
5,6. *open questions*

12. Cookery class

Sheet **12b**:
1. chocolate, marshmallows, chocolate beans
2. wash and dry hands
3. break chocolate up
4. leave to set
5. in case don't have everything

Year 4 Term 2

13. The class garden

Sheet **13b**:
1. Tools: wheelbarrow, spade, rake
   Advice: parents, site agent, garden centre, books, internet
   Helpers: other children
2. as one sort dies, another sort blooms, so it is always colourful
3. dig, weed, push wheelbarrow, plant, water

Sheet **13c**:
1. site agent, parents, friends, books, internet
2. water
3. watering, weeding; take turns to do work during holidays?
4. garden centres, flower shops, adults, books, internet
5. *open question*

14. Staying alive

Sheet **14a**: *open questions*

15. The largest lizard

Sheet **15b**:
1. Komodo dragon
2. 3m
3. no
4. Indonesia, Komodo Island
5. won't find one in our country, probably dangerous

Sheet **15c**:
1. largest known lizard in world; heavy body; long tail; very strong claws
2. up to 3m long; doesn't blow smoke; doesn't breath fire
3. frightening size
4. no – only lives in Indonesia
5. author wants us to stop and think about each piece of information because so interesting

Year 4 Term 3

16. Making you buy

Sheet **16b**:
1. Pretty: new; hottest magazine; for pretty girls so makes you feel pretty when buy it; hair, beauty, fashion tips; how to meet trendiest friends; might win cash; lotsa – trendy word; free lipstick
   Kidz: trendiest gear; "clothes with wow!"; baseball cap – buy one get one free

2. Pretty: for pretty mums; daughters will be popular; might win cash; free lipstick
   Kidz: children will like clothes; not expensive; baseball cap – buy one get one free

17. Advertising

Sheet **17b**:
1. a) miracle, markle, makes
   b) slendo, slimmer
   c) dofo, delicious, dog
   d) bebu, best, butter, buy, bread, better
2. we don't know all dogs like it
3. short for <u>dog</u> <u>food</u>
4. Markle, sparkle; whiter, brighter
5–7. *open questions*

Sheet **17c**:
1. *open question*
2. *see sheet* **17b**, *1.*
3. washing can't sparkle; Slendo can't make you slimmer, only look it; we don't know all dogs like Dofo; no evidence Bebu is best butter
4. price
5. funny spellings, bold lettering, pictures, rhyme, alliteration, funny nonsense words

18. Too many words

Sheet **18a**:
1. look carefully both ways
2. listen
3. be careful around parked cars

Sheet **18b**:
1. good for me: fruit, vegetables, salad, rice, pasta, whole grain foods, porridge
   not good for me: pastries, cakes, sweets, chips, burgers, sausage rolls, crisps, fizzy drinks
   advice: clean teeth regularly, change toothbrush regularly
2. *open question*

Answers to worksheets

Year 5 Term 1

19. Reporting

Sheet **19a**:
1. Corry Football Stadium
2. four
3. Black
4. Jamal
5. excellent shot

Sheet **19b**:
1. diary
2. girl
3. young
4. Friday
5. Mandy
6. no – not necessary to include routine activities
7. writer of diary
8. remind her of things

Sheet **19c**:
1. police officer
2. written in report
3. Mr Armstrong parking car in front of Mr Browne's gate
4. report used as evidence later

20. Breakfast made easy

Sheet **20a**
1. *open question*
2. don't have all ingredients; no microwave or toaster
3. *open question*

21. The holiday

Sheet **21a**:
1. Lake District
2. £250
3. pay in instalments

Sheet **21b**:
1. a) Lake District
   b) £250
   c) adult to every five children
   d) pay in instalments
   e) sleeping bag, pillow cases, towels, equipment for chosen activity

2. parents need to know things, notes remind us of details

Year 5 Term 2

22. Little Red Riding Hood

Sheet **22a**:
1. "All the better to hear you with.", "All the better to see you with.", "All the better to eat you with!"
2. snarls, leaps out of bed

Sheet **22b**: *open activity*

23. Houses for sale

Sheet **23b**:
1. Wilson Avenue: space, big garden, quiet street, close to schools
2. Parkington Crescent: ground floor, quiet area, small, easily kept garden, close to shops and public transport
3. Gloucester Street: no lift, not too big, good view
4. Wilson Avenue: too big

24. The new hall

Sheet **24a**:
1. yes
2. yes
3. games, dancing, football, netball, entertainment, plays
4. ramp
5. slide shows, films, plays

Sheet **24b**:
hall, wooden, dancing, made, football, piano, curtains, toilets, steps, ramp

Sheet **24c**: *open activity*

Year 5 Term 3

25. Letters to the editor

Sheet **25b**: *open activity*

Sheet **25c**:
1. Give information: A, C, D
   Give opinion: A, B, C
   Persuade: A, C
   Complain: A, B
2. *open activity*

26. The flyer

Sheet **26a**:
1. easy way to learn to dance
2. how you learn, price
3. draw attention to good things, play down other things
4. say not used product properly
5. feel foolish, blame yourself

Sheet **26b**:
1. feel better, look better, think better, probably live longer; two capsules a day change life
2. price, ingredients, side effects
3. negative things put you off
4. feel foolish
5. might, convinced, use properly, short time, confident, probably, could

27. Persuasive words and phrases

Sheet **27b**:
1. popular so must be good; we don't know nobody can resist it
2. opinion; we don't know every girl in world
3. in case you don't like it – allows them to say it's the best
4. supposed recommendation of professionals; we don't know all professionals use ball

Sheet **27d**:
1. renown, trusted; we don't know about whole world
2. implies if you believe it you're not intelligent
3. you think you're caring, so you feel obliged to give
4. we don't know all professionals use it
5. no evidence

Answers to worksheets

Year 6 Term 1

28. My pop star life

Sheet **28c**:
1. *open question*
2. make himself more interesting, get sympathy from fans
3. sound exciting, original
4,5. *open questions*

Sheet **28d**:
1. biography: **28b**
   autobiography: **28a**
2. poor area – many people living close together, not peaceful
3. comfortable, plenty of money
4–6. *open questions*

29. Sports report

Sheet **29b**:
1. *open question*
2. driving seat, wrap up, came alive, poached, sweet, grab control, drained, unlocked, cracking
3. interest, excite reader
4. where/when races were, how many competed in, how exciting/close they were, prize

30. Granton School football club

Sheet **30b**:
1. meet on Mondays after school
2. a) fit
   b) friends
   c) other students
3. a) strips
   b) equipment
   c) expenses
4. raise funds for them

Sheet **30c**:
1. meet on Mondays after school
2. yes
3. yes; "success rate is high"
4. keep fit, make friends, travel to meet other students
5. no
6. *open question*
7. raise funds for them

Year 6 Term 2

31. School uniform

Sheet **31c**:
1. dull and boring
2. expensive; could buy cheaper clothes
3. could be traced to school
4. *open question*

Sheet **31d**:
1–3. *see sheet 31c, 1–3.*
4. knows what to wear each day; warm; comfortable
5. if you're proud of your school, you should wear its uniform
6. you couldn't afford expensive clothes like them
7. can wear what you like every evening, at weekends
8,9. *open questions*

32. Staying out late at night

Sheet **32b**:
1. most youth clubs don't finish until 8pm; can't chat to friends; could lose them; safe at that time
2. only twelve; too young to defend herself; lots of homework to do; swimming lesson early on Saturday
3. nearly thirteen
4. only twelve
5. *open question*

Sheet **32c**:
1,2. *see sheet 32b 1,2.*
3–5. *open questions*

Year 6 Term 3

33. Putting it bluntly

Sheet **33d**:
1. first
2. angry about people coming in late, wants to stop it
3. explains problem, asks workers to be on time rather than threatening them, language less formal

4. allowed, put up with
5. the sack
6. *open question*

Sheet **33e**:
1. first
2. **33b** explains why debt is a problem, more friendly, informal
3. a) iv; b) iii; c) i; d) v; e) ii
4. impersonal: **33a**
   personal: **33b**
5. highest amount you can have

34. Crossing the road

Sheet **34b**:
people, malaria, tuberculosis, Today, children, countries, developing/poorer, rise/increase/go up, Organization, twice, roads, traffic, 1896, coroner, happen

Sheet **34c**:
1. malaria, tuberculosis
2. as deadly as malaria and tuberculosis; 3000 people die per day, including 500 children; number of people hurt in accidents in poorer countries is going up; will be at least twice as many deaths on roads by 2020
3. we're aware now of need to wear seatbelts and obey speed limits; be seen, cross roads carefully, wear helmet, don't drink and drive
4. poor quality roads, old vehicles, traffic rules ignored
5–7. *open questions*

35. Different types of texts

Sheet **35b**:
1. dictionary, encyclopedia, medical book
2. catalogue, shop window, newspaper
3. dictionary
4. notice board in school/college
5. colour, texture, shape, size
6. free – to attract customers

Printed in the United Kingdom
by Lightning Source UK Ltd.
115654UKS00001B/7-106